Guide to

So

D0439386

A Guide to South Carolina Beaches

William W. Starr

UNIVERSITY OF SOUTH CAROLINA PRESS

UNIVERSITY OF SOUTH CAROLINA *BICENTENNIAL*

© 2001 University of South Carolina

Published in Columbia, South Carolina, by the
University of South Carolina Press

Manufactured in the United States of America

05 04 03 02 01   5 4 3 2 1

Library of Congress Cataloging-in-Publication Data

Starr, William W., 1940-
  A guide to South Carolina beaches / William W. Starr.
    p. cm.
Includes bibliographical references and index.
  ISBN 1-57003-432-X (pbk. : alk. paper)
  1. South Carolina—Guidebooks. 2. Beaches—South Carolina—Guidebooks.
  I. Title.
  F267.3 .S73 2001
  917.5704′44—dc21   2001002086

For my very special family:
Amy, Matthew, Francis, Radostina, Heidi,
Karl, Erik, Pam, Page, and especially Carol.
Thanks for everything, time and again.

Contents

Illustrations

Maps created by Rob Barge

Acknowledgments

A book like this doesn't get done without the aid and encouragement of a great many people. My list begins with Catherine Fry at the University of South Carolina Press, who had the idea, the patience, and the push to make it come together. Without her, I'd still be hiking the mountains. I'm grateful, too, for the small army of people who functioned as scouts, advisors, snoops, hand-holders, and information-sharers. Those who work in South Carolina's tourist industry have been most generous with their time and assistance, whether handling my telephone requests, providing material, or guiding me firsthand through parts of this magnificent coast. Thanks certainly go to the South Carolina Department of Parks, Recreation and Tourism for their help in securing illustrations. The early readers of this book supplied a wealth of up-to-date information and subtleties that I recall with gratitude. And Linda Haines Fogle and Barbara Brannon at USC Press asked just the right questions and applied just the right touches to keep the project focused. All of those who aided me merit the highest accolades. None deserve any of the blame for errors of judgment or fact that may occur here; those are solely the responsibility of the author.

Of course, a book such as this one cannot be up-to-date in all respects. The process of revising, adding, and subtracting has continued almost simultaneously with the writing of these chapters. Readers should know every effort has been made to incorporate changes at the last minute before publication. But humans are as fickle as nature; as the coast itself is reshaped by the tide every twenty-four hours, so too do humans create their own ebb and flow. Keeping track of that remains a challenging twenty-four-hour-a-day task, albeit it a fun one.

Introduction

Ask anyone who's ever spent time there and you'll quickly discover why the South Carolina coast is such an extraordinarily distinctive environment, and why hardly anyone ever goes to there without vowing to return. It carries a rich history and secrets both wonderful and perverse. Much of it is as hauntingly beautiful as any place on earth. Parts of it testify to humanity's shortsightedness and lack of vision. Curiously, those conflicting elements can and do coexist almost within the same mile marker.

From Little River at the northernmost boundary of the South Carolina coast to Daufuskie Island at the southern end—the path this book follows—the coast snakes its way though a pattern of marsh grass, dunes, sand, and inlets, all shaped by the waters of the Atlantic Ocean. It's been that way for centuries, for humans are the newcomers here. Yet man's mark is seemingly everywhere, from the tour boats that ply the dark, silent waterways to the high-rises of Myrtle Beach, from the swaying sea oats at Pawleys Island to the golf course bustle of Hilton Head Island, from the millionaire's homes at Kiawah Island to the rickety wood frame apartments at Windy Hill Beach.

But there is so much more. Sit on a lonely beach as a summer storm sweeps ashore and marvel at the mighty collision of natural forces. Maybe even see a real ghost; there are several on the coast, you know, and one of them is even a welcome herald for bad weather. Sit on a Palmetto log, half buried in sand, and observe the dazzling interplay of beach life. Walk through some of America's most gorgeous beaches and laugh at the beads of sand that cling warmly to your ankle. There is something special and thrilling about these coastal places which awaits your own discovery.

I've been hanging around the coast for more than fifty years. There aren't many places I haven't walked through, played in, rested on, or eaten in. And I'd like to think I might be granted another fifty years to do the same. Of course, the coast has changed, but then so have I. Once the lure of excitement at night drew me; now the solitude of the day intrigues me. It pleases me greatly to know that the coast offers so many choices for so many people. It is chameleonlike in a sense, a shape-shifter if you will, offering up what you most wish it to give you. To reap that gift, however, you will need to know more about the coast. Understanding enriches your knowledge. It is my hope that this book may, in at least some way, be a guide to your discovery, your adventure, and your deepest wish fulfillment.

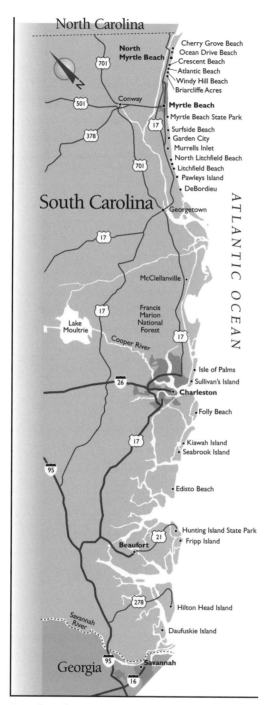

Maps by Rob Barge

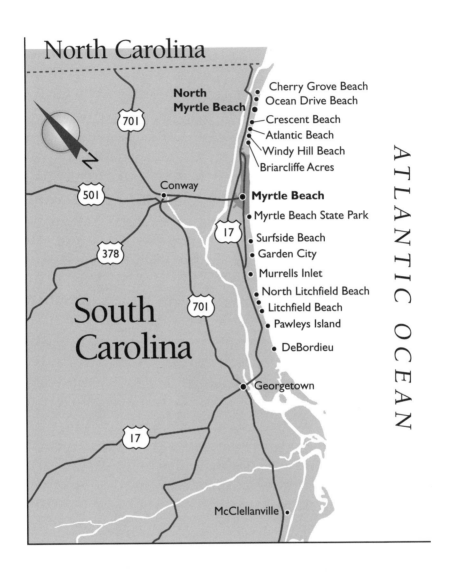

North Carolina

North
Myrtle Beach

Cherry Grove Beach
Ocean Drive Beach
Crescent Beach
Atlantic Beach
Windy Hill Beach
Briarcliffe Acres

701

501

Conway

Myrtle Beach

Myrtle Beach State Park

17

Surfside Beach

Garden City

378

Murrells Inlet

North Litchfield Beach

701

Litchfield Beach

Pawleys Island

DeBordieu

South
Carolina

Georgetown

17

McClellanville

ATLANTIC OCEAN

One

Myrtle Beach and the Grand Strand

North

Anyone in search of sun, surf, and sand who has a hankering to rev it up when the sun goes down can't miss Myrtle Beach. It's a magnet with enough energy and activity to drive a bus full of social directors bonkers. No kidding: If you can't find anything to do in Myrtle Beach, your dark glasses need lightening. This is Baghdad on the Waccamaw. Grab your suntan lotion and c'mon down.

The mere mention of Myrtle Beach produces an instant reaction. It either makes your heart beat a little faster or gives you a feeling of mild indigestion. It all depends on what you're looking for, though to judge by the crowds in the early years of the new millennium, there are a lot more hearts racing than folks reaching for the antacids.

Myrtle Beach exerts an appeal to all levels of tastes and pocketbooks. It has it all, including a wonderful white sand beach, although sometimes that can get overlooked in the crush of traffic, golf, shows, shopping, and construction. It's nirvana for some 13.5 million people every year, from Canada to Connecticut, from Charlotte to Cincinnati. It's the most popular destination on the East Coast after Atlantic City's casinos and Orlando's Walt Disney World. It's got a lot of the glitz of Atlantic City (and better beaches), though the gambling casinos are on boats floating offshore. And it's got some of the amusement-park feel of Disney World (albeit without Mickey). It's a summer melting pot—literally in the temperatures and figuratively in the throngs of sunburned bodies—and there's no place remotely like it between Nantucket and Miami. It's a mecca for golfers year-round. It's a lure for vacationers hungry for shopping and entertainment. And it's beset with traffic jams that can make New York's street grids seem like an expressway.

It's exciting, frustrating, over-the-top, beautiful, tacky, delicious, hilarious, contemporary, draining, nonstop, bold, endless. And it has more miniature golf courses than any other place in the semi-civilized world. So if you want beige, quiet, calm, and easygoing, take yourself somewhere else. This is choice city, and hey, McDonald's made it by selling more than hamburgers, right?

Myrtle Beach is actually more than just Myrtle Beach. It's the centerpiece of the Grand Strand, a sixty-mile stretch of beach that gently curves from Little River at the North Carolina state line down to Georgetown on the south side. The Grand Strand encompasses more than a dozen different beach communities, including Myrtle Beach itself, the populous heartbeat of the this colorful coastal landscape. Some of these beaches have very distinct personalities.

Pawleys Island on the south end of the Strand, for instance, is the antithesis of everything Myrtle Beach represents and darned proud of it. The Pawleys slogan, "Arrogantly Shabby," throws its challenge into the face of new timeshares, condos, and high-rises in relentlessly ambitious Myrtle Beach. But nearly all of the communities ultimately take their cue in one way or another from Myrtle Beach, and for marketing purposes, are all part of the Grand Strand package. What they have in common, apart from coastal location, is golf courses and seafood restaurants.

The Grand Strand boasts more than 100 golf courses, which breaks down facetiously to about one hole per permanent resident. It also permits over 3 million rounds of golf here each year, which makes this area America's second most popular golf destination after Florida. The layouts are some of the very best in the nation. They were designed by the legendary likes of Jack Nicklaus, Tom Fazio, Arnold Palmer, Robert Trent Jones, Pete Dye . . . well, you get the idea. There is no place in America where so many outstanding courses are so closely linked. Golfers could play eighteen holes twice a day and still not be close to running out of courses by the end of a month. The agreeable year-round weather (well, yes, it does get hot in summer) means the courses beckon at all seasons. And the layouts, whether capitalizing on beach or marsh landscape, are among the most attractive anywhere.

And when golfers finish their rounds, along with everyone else at the beach, it's time to hit the restaurants. No one apparently has ever definitively calculated the number of eating establishments along the Grand Strand, but the estimates are they number about 2,000. Which means, conservatively

The Grand Strand stretches for sixty miles from Little River to Georgetown, bringing some 13.5 million visitors a year to its white sand beaches and Southern hospitality. (Courtesy Myrtle Beach Area Chamber of Commerce)

speaking, that if all the fried shrimp consumed on the Strand on one hot evening in July were laid end to end, they would stretch from Pawleys to Petrograd and back again. And we haven't even mentioned hush puppies yet. The relatively inexpensive cuisine is locally known as Calabash style, which is basically all manner of seafood, some of it caught in these waters, battered and fried and served with French fries and iced tea or cold beer. Great dining, no, but try it and you'll almost certainly come away fat and happy.

Shopaholics are in trouble in Myrtle Beach and the Strand. It's not just that there are some really cool stores and shops and malls and discounters, but that there are so many of them. We're not just talking outlet malls selling beach towels and suntan lotion but some of the country's biggest and best-known retailers: the likes of J. Crew, L. L. Bean, Ralph Lauren, Gucci, and some of their acquaintances. Anyone who helicopters over the Strand shouldn't be astonished to see the malls as busy as the beaches during the day.

And when the sun finally drops off, there's the entertainment. In the last decade, the Strand has blossomed as a haven for nightlife mavens. Some call it "Branson East," a reference to the small Missouri town that has put itself on the map as a home for numerous pop/country performers. Myrtle Beach, however, is much larger than Branson in every way, though the appeal to many vacationers is every bit as compelling. From dark bars oozing a beery smell to

By day or by night, visitors can feel the rush of amusement rides at several parks in Myrtle Beach. Some are wet and wild, and some are just plain wild. (Courtesy South Carolina Department of Parks, Recreation & Tourism)

noisy, mammoth, cheery clubs like Hard Rock Café and Planet Hollywood, from tiny venues hosting a young guitarist trying his talent to multi-thousand-seat complexes spotlighting Broadway shows like *Cats*, the Strand attracts tens of thousands of evening-outers every night. Elderly vacationers mingle with family groups hauling toddlers and teenagers on the make. On summer weekends, the crush can be staggering—sometimes literally, not figuratively. The last person to depart Myrtle Beach complaining about nothing to do at night passed away last year in an old folk's home.

It hasn't always been like that, of course.

Way back when, say around 1526, Spanish adventurers established the first settlement in North America on Winyah Bay near Georgetown on the south end of the Grand Strand. That was nearly a century before the English founded Jamestown in Virginia in 1607 and some 14,000 years after human beings are known to have been residing in the area. For unknown reasons, but probably having something to do with Native Americans who were less than thrilled at the aggressive disturbance, the Spanish drop-by did not last long.

The English founded the first permanent European settlement in South Carolina in 1670 in the area around present-day Charleston (about 100 miles south of Myrtle Beach). Soon afterward a culture of rice-growing built on the labor and knowledge of black slaves developed along the coastal areas as far north as Brookgreen Gardens, just to the south of Myrtle Beach, providing a means of great wealth for a handful of white planters.

Because much of the area around modern-day Myrtle Beach and inland was swampy and dense with tupelo gum and cypress trees, the plantations did not expand into the region. It was settled, instead, by hardy Scotch-Irish farmers whose one-mule lands dominated until near the turn of the last century. Timber-clearing operations opened a way to the coast, and the tiny community of Myrtle Beach acquired its name in 1900 for a native shrub, not much in evidence these days amid the bustle of a growing resort. The first resort hotel opened in 1901.

(This is perhaps a good time to insert a historical aside that might save you possible embarrassment. Myrtle Beach is located in Horry County, which is not pronounced the way you think it might be. The correct way, according to a pair of South Carolina experts on that sort of thing, the late Claude Henry Neuffer and his wife Irene, is OH-REE. The H is silent. It's named for an officer in the American Revolution, Peter Horry. In the Neuffers' popular book, *Correct Mispronunciations of Some South Carolina Names,* they described some Northern visitors to Charleston years ago who were looking for Colonel Horry's house. The tourists stopped an older woman to ask for directions to the HO-ri house and were sharply advised to watch their language because children were nearby. This story may or may not be apocryphal, but it will prevent you from immediately being labeled as an outsider.)

The first road (dirt, naturally) to Myrtle Beach in 1914 opened the way for accelerated growth, and the construction of the Ocean Forest Hotel in the next decade seemed to herald boom times. The Depression, however, followed by World War II, kept Myrtle Beach from expanding rapidly, and it was not until the 1950s, after the damage of Hurricane Hazel in 1954, that the Grand Strand began drawing attention as an important tourist destination.

The construction of golf courses cleared the way for a quantum leap in crowds by the mid-1970s, and the construction of everything else—high-rise condos, hotels, motels, timeshares, apartments, resorts, restaurants, stores, shops—followed. And the trend hasn't stopped, or slowed, since. The Grand Strand is only getting larger.

On a busy midsummer weekend, The sixty miles from Little River to Georgetown can bulge with hundreds of thousands of vacationers who come this way each year. On the busiest holiday weekends, perhaps as many as half a million people fill the Grand Strand. The year-round population of the city of Myrtle Beach is just a little over 30,000, but when you add up all the numbers you have the largest conglomeration of people in South Carolina and the busiest metropolitan area in the state. Anyone who's been in the middle of it on the Fourth of July will have no doubts.

The roads to Myrtle Beach are paved with cars. Getting to and around the beach on summer weekends is harder than pushing a termite through a jar of honey. And just about as sticky. The primary entrance to Myrtle Beach is on Highway 501 from Conway, a four-lane road obsolete a decade ago and incapable of handling the crush of traffic now. North-south routes on Highway 17 into the beach area are not much better, and the bypass already is choked with cars. The many shopping and entertainment complexes create their own traffic blocks, and the result, especially on summer weekends, is long lines of stalled cars and trucks with everybody getting hotter (and not just from the thermometer). The state of South Carolina is opening new roads like Highway 22 to improve the flow—or perhaps, to create a flow—but for the short term, visitors should pack patience along with swimsuits and water bottles.

Getting Oriented

Because it sprawls along the coast for sixty miles, a very gentle curve from the northeast to the southwest that includes an eclectic if not spectroscopic assortment of beach communities, the Grand Strand requires getting to know a bit geographically.

The Strand is like a very long island. Separating its beaches from the inland areas is the Intracoastal Waterway, which spans the Atlantic Seaboard and provides a calm passage for boats away from the ocean. A little south of Myrtle Beach, the Waterway moves into the Waccamaw River, which flows into the Atlantic at Georgetown, the southern anchor of the Strand. To the east of the Waterway are the beaches; to the west, inland.

US Highway 17 is the main thoroughfare, which bisects the Strand. There are signs pointing to specific beaches along the way, but be careful: The signs are not always easy to locate, especially if you're unfamiliar with the way and are caught in heavy traffic. If you're driving on a beachfront road, one community can blend into the next almost imperceptibly. One moment you're driving in Cherry Grove Beach, the next you're in Ocean Drive Beach without realizing it. It can be a little confusing. But all of the beaches to the north and south of Myrtle Beach are considerably less densely packed with people and structures than Myrtle Beach proper.

Starting at the top of the curve and moving north to south, here's a brief look at the beaches and communities that make up the Strand.

Little River

Starting at the North Carolina state line at the uppermost limits of the Strand is the charming fishing village of Little River. This isn't a beach, but from here visitors can book a deep-sea fishing trip or a boating excursion or put their own boat in the water at a public landing. And there's another type of on-water activity here as well: a "cruise to nowhere."

That's what they call the gambling boats that sail from here just about every day of the year. Though gambling is illegal in South Carolina, the state has a colorful history of gambling activities. Voters in the 2000 election approved establishment of a state lottery, but well before that in the nineteenth century there were horse races and cockfights, and bets were placed by slaves and slaveowners alike. Bible Belt it may be, but gambling seems to be near to the heart of many South Carolinians, too.

At Little River, a pair of casino boats carry gamblers offshore a few miles into legal waters and then offer blackjack, roulette, poker, craps, and slots. There are cruises that last for several hours, and some others include dinner. You don't need advance reservations; you can sign up at the casino offices at Little River. Be aware, however, that legal efforts to suppress gambling surface in the legislature from time to time, so this activity is subject to interruptions without a lot of advance notice.

The official South Carolina state welcome center, staffed seven days a week during daylight hours, is located near Little River off US Highway 17 at the South Carolina–North Carolina state line, and workers there can advise travelers on the latest gambling news as well as point the way to a host of attractions up and down the Grand Strand. The center carries a wealth of informational materials about all of South Carolina and is well worth a stop. If you need help finding a place to stay, the staffers here also can assist with that.

Apart from the notoriety of gambling, Little River is a lovely little community with a few shops set amid ancient, weathered oaks that create an ambience which, if not quite as laid-back as it used to be—and remember, George Washington dined near here during his 1791 visit—still isn't matched at many other spots along the Strand. Check out the fun and food at the Crab Festival here in May. And if you want to eat where the locals eat, drop by the Admiral's Flagship Restaurant. Nothing fancy, but lots of good seafood. The Calabash-style restaurants offer all kinds of fresh seafood. Accommodations include bed-and-breakfasts, efficiencies, and some small motels.

Cherry Grove Beach

One of several beach areas part of North Myrtle Beach, Cherry Grove is a family beach offering a variety of housing choices, from new moderate-rise condos to considerably older homes beside the serpentine marshes and inlets. Lots of food outlets are nearby. There's plenty of good crabbing here, and surf fishing, too.

Ocean Drive Beach

FOR INFORMATION about Ocean Drive and other North Myrtle Beach locations, call (877) 332-2662 or visit nmyrtlebeachchamber.org.
. . . .

Continuing south brings you to one of the best-known beaches in the area, Ocean Drive. Known to many as simply "OD," it was here that generations of young beachgoers learned what is now the official South Carolina state dance, the shag. (There's also an official state rock, a state insect, and a state amphibian, if you're curious. The rock is blue granite, the insect is the Carolina Mantid, and the amphibian is the ever-popular spotted salamander.) The dance originated in the late 1940s and early '50s and was made popular at a nightclub called The Pad, which closed after a fire in 1987 and was demolished in 1994. There are now, however, other clubs where you can learn or practice the shag. The dance steps off to boogie harmonies and involves moving rhythmically a lot below the waist while holding yourself stiff above. It helps, say aficionados, if you can look a little bored while you're doing it, and some of its numerous practitioners claim an occasional cold beer helps loosen the limbs in just the right way. Fat Harold's Beach Club is among the best-known establishments where you can get into some upscale shagging. There's an annual S.O.S. (Society of Stranders) event in the fall here that brings thousands of fans together for a long weekend of partying. As with Cherry Grove, there is a diverse selection of accommodations, including a high-rise hotel and golf resort. The prices are diverse too, no matter your shagging skills.

Crescent Beach

FOR INFORMATION about Crescent Beach, call (877) 332-2662 or visit nmyrtlebeachchamber.org.
. . . .

Like its neighbors to the north, Crescent Beach is a part of the North Myrtle Beach umbrella and is considered a good family beach, quieter and less hectic than Myrtle Beach but a relatively short drive away from the action if the urge comes over you. It also has a variety of lodgings for visitors, from a number of older homes to apartments to a scattering of motels and commercial establishments.

Atlantic Beach

Atlantic Beach is a little bit different on several counts. It is a part of the North Myrtle Beach area, but it is incorporated as a separate municipality. In the era of segregation in the South, it was the only beach along a large part of the South Atlantic that was open and hospitable to black families. And thousands of blacks from the Carolinas, Georgia, and Florida spent parts of their summer here. It had its own town officials and operated unto itself, exerting a special tug on the hearts of many thousands of African Americans, most of whom were denied the use of the state's public beaches.

Its current physical environment is the subject of several revitalization efforts in an attempt to bring new life to this once-active community. The historical importance of Atlantic Beach cannot be overstated, however, and a reminder of its status is evidenced by the old natural blockades preventing travelers on the beachfront road from easily connecting to the formerly white-only beaches on either side. An access road off US 17 is the route to the beach. Old-timers here speak lovingly of its past and look hungrily to a future of improved facilities.

Windy Hill

FOR INFORMATION about windy Hill, call (877) 332-2662 or visit nmyrtlebeachchamber.org.

••

Perhaps the least developed of the beach communities north of Myrtle Beach is Windy Hill. Smaller in size, too, it has a range of older housing options for weekend or week-long renters. It has long been a popular stop for families, some of whom have been coming here for generations, taking pleasure from its quiet, easygoing atmosphere, a striking contrast to the bright lights and entertainment only a few miles to the south in Myrtle Beach itself.

Briarcliffe Acres

Briarcliffe Acres—which might sound like the setting for a television sitcom—is actually a small, upscale, residential, incorporated community. By design, there's not much for visitors here, and its location is appropriately not easy to find. (It's just about across US 17 from the large Briarcliffe Mall.)

Myrtle Beach

Myrtle Beach is the center of the coastal universe for hundreds of thousands of visitors, the most populous and popular of South Carolina's beaches. It you can't find it here, you probably wouldn't want it anyway. Over the last decade, various national rating services have proclaimed it the "Hottest New Destination" and among the "Top Ten Best Family Destinations."

If you're looking for a place to stay, there are 40,000 rooms here to fit all sizes of pocketbooks and families, from the lowliest mom-and-pop motel to the fanciest high-rise condo or hotel. Prices range just as much, from $39 a night (getting harder to find) upwards to hundreds of dollars. Stay by the night, by the weekend, by the week, by the month. No problem. There are more than 7,000 campground spaces in the Myrtle Beach area for RVs or tents, whatever your preference. And if you get hungry, there probably are more restaurants than lodgings around here, everything from a hamburger to a six-course dinner with mostly in-between. Golf—regular or miniature—abounds. Huge entertainment complexes pocket the landscape. Nightlife is a dazzling swirl of choices. Shopping centers are as ubiquitous as sand fleas and can do even more damage to your wallet. Traffic can be stress-inducing if you're trying to get somewhere quickly, especially in downtown Myrtle Beach or on the roads leading in and out of the area. Like it or hate it, Myrtle Beach is unique and a unique draw, and like a magnet it draws from its neighbors to the north and south.

Among those lured to the area in very large and growing numbers are motorcyclists. In the middle of May each year, the Harley-Davidson Bike Week brings an estimated 100,000 cyclists from all over the country into Myrtle Beach and the Strand. And on Memorial Day weekend, African American cyclists make an annual sojourn to the Atlantic Beach area on the north Strand. Together, those arrivals can add delays to an already congested highway system along the beach, so anyone headed for Myrtle Beach at those times should be prepared. The bikers, by the way, also add plenty of money to the beach economy during their stay, and insiders say they are among the best tippers at restaurants any time of year.

Before 1954, Myrtle Beach was a popular resort but known mostly to residents of South Carolina and North Carolina. Then Hurricane Hazel struck the area, causing extensive damage and creating an urban renewal explosion that brought Myrtle Beach back bigger and better than ever. Within a decade,

If camping is your idea of vacation heaven, you'll find everything from full hookups to tent sites to cabins in the Myrtle Beach area. (Courtesy Myrtle Beach Area Chamber of Commerce)

it was beginning to lure visitors from much farther away, and by the 1970s the sound of construction was matched only by the sound of cash registers and money being spent. Myrtle Beach has grown out and up, and no one looks back any more. See the end of this section for sources of information about Myrtle Beach.

Myrtle Beach State Park

FOR INFORMATION call (843) 238-5325 or visit the state parks website at www.southcarolinaparks.com.

• •

South Carolina enjoys a terrific state park system boasting some of the finest beaches along the Atlantic coast. The parks are inexpensive to use, accessible and darned beautiful places. Anyone looking for a beach experience for just a day shouldn't miss them, and many vacationers with a week or two along the coast make it a point to spend a little time here, too. The 312-acre Myrtle Beach State Park, about three miles south of the Myrtle Beach downtown area off US 17, is the state's oldest state park. There's plenty of oceanfront for sand, sun, and surf and even pool swimming, too. There are 350 camping sites and several cabins and apartments (which are very difficult to find empty in summer). Visitors can enjoy pier or surf fishing, stroll through the nature trail, or just rest in the shade and savor a picnic lunch. Although it's in the middle of the busy and under-construction Grand Strand, the park remains an uncommonly quiet and attractive natural area. There is a small admission fee.

It's probably a good idea to understand the basics of reserving spaces through the state park system because they are so busy in summer and so popular year-round. Briefly, there are cabins for use at Myrtle Beach, Edisto Beach, and Hunting Island State Parks. They rent by the week only, Monday to Monday, during the summer months. Call on the first Monday following January 1 of each year to make your reservation. If you delay at all, you'll almost certainly be out of luck. Out of the summer season, the cabins receive heavy use, but nightly rentals are at least offered for the rest of the year.

You can call up to eleven months in advance to reserve one of the camping sites at Myrtle Beach, Huntington Beach, or Hunting Island State Parks. But many of the sites are not available for advance reservations; the state parks system keeps most of them open on a daily first-come, first-served basis. So get there early if it's July and you need a place to camp.

Visiting the Grand Strand

Weather

There are few surprises here. The average January high is 59° F and the low is 40°. In mid-summer, average highs are 89° F and lows 74°. The rainfall in January averages about 4 inches; in July it's about 6.5 inches. The thermometer climbs into the 90s in the summer months, often extending into September. Humidities are high, too, which is why people get in the water a lot. Occasionally it's even hotter, but there's usually relief in the breezes coming off the ocean. The occasional late afternoon thunderstorm can help cool things off a little. The rest of the year the temperature is moderate, which helps account for the tremendous popularity of golf. If you don't mind the summer heat, golf is a twelve-month activity in the Grand Strand. Spring and fall temperatures are perfect for hitting the links or anything else outdoors (and the water temperatures in fall are delightfully warm, too). In winter, it can be chilly, once in a while cold when the ocean breezes seem relentless. But cold days are often followed by very mild ones, and the outdoors beckons to sweater-wearers. And yes, as unlikely as it might seem, Myrtle Beach has experienced occasional snow in winter, but don't bet your vacation savings on it happening while you're there. The only reason you'll want a sweater in summer is to feel comfortable in chilled-down restaurants.

Getting Around

The beach is made for walking; the Grand Strand is made for driving. A car is essential if you're going to get around beyond your immediate location. Remember, we're talking sixty miles here. Everything is spread out, and to go from a motel to a restaurant to a shopping center and on to a golf course can cover many miles. Admittedly, though, the traffic can be so overwhelming at times as to make it seem that walking would be faster. Never mind; you'll need a car. If you don't arrive in one, you can easily rent one at the Myrtle Beach International Airport or at other locations around the Strand; ask at your place of lodging. Rates are not high, and vehicles are plentiful. Air conditioning comes with rental cars, and you'll be glad it does. There are taxis, but they are comparatively expensive, and you may not enjoy watching the meter run while you stew in traffic.

Day-trippers will find small free public parking areas scattered along the Strand's oceanfront streets. Each lot usually accommodates no more than a handful of vehicles, so if one is filled drive several blocks farther down Ocean Boulevard, and you'll find another. There's no time limit on the parking, and the lots have a direct beach access path.

It's important to understand the layout of the principal roadways in the Strand to know how to cope with the traffic flow in this busy area. Remember that the main roads parallel the Atlantic Ocean. Ocean Boulevard is closest to the ocean. It runs north to south, from Cherry Grove Beach in the north to Surfside Beach south of Myrtle Beach. Alas, it is does not run continuously and is broken in several places (at Myrtle Beach State Park and Atlantic Beach, for instance) before picking up a few miles away. Lots of hotels and motels obviously are found here, including beachfront properties, so there will be lots of pedestrians and slow-moving traffic since everyone likes to cruise and rubberneck.

Moving inland, the next major road paralleling the ocean is four-lane US 17, also known as Business 17 or King's Highway. The artery runs from Little River at the top of the Grand Strand to Georgetown at the south end and beyond that to Charleston. As the name suggests, it is lined with businesses and traffic lights and will require time and patience to negotiate. It's easy to follow, however, and there are signs pointing to the beach exits.

The next important road inland is the well-marked four-lane Highway 17 Bypass which—you guessed it—dodges US 17. It runs between Murrells Inlet and North Myrtle Beach. There are traffic lights scattered along the bypass. And since it passes some of the major entertainment and shopping complexes it can be a traffic bottleneck on weekend afternoon and evenings no matter the season.

The traffic is lighter the farther away from Myrtle Beach you drive on these roads. South of Pawleys Island heading into Georgetown, US 17 becomes much less crowded. There are no traffic lights and few retail establishments along the sides of the highway and your chances of reaching the 55-mile-an-hour speed limit increase greatly.

Driving east and west into and out of Myrtle Beach is problematic. Which is a charitable way of saying you've got a better chance of observing jellyfish roadkill than avoiding delays. The principal artery leading to the beach is US 501, which connects the city of Conway to Myrtle Beach. It is four lanes wanting eight. Hundreds of thousands of people arrive and depart the Grand Strand on this road every year, and the worst times are found on Saturdays and Sundays. The highway is lined with every conceivable sort of retail establishment, so lots of people are trying to get in and off it in addition to drivers headed to either Conway or Myrtle Beach.

If you've left Conway for Myrtle Beach and your eventual destination is to the south end of the Strand, you can turn right on State Road 544 between Conway and Myrtle Beach which will connect up with the 17 Bypass. Or keep going on 501 until you get to the bypass and then exit to the right. Highway 544 is two lanes and can be very slow, but then, it can be slow going just getting to the bypass.

If your destination is the North Myrtle Beach area, there's a new road to ease you past some of the worst travel on 501. Between Aynor and Conway, look for the exit off 501 to Highway 22. This 28-mile stretch will take you directly into the North Myrtle Beach vicinity at Highway 17. It's definitely a big improvement if you're headed toward the beach on 501, or if you're leaving the beach area headed home.

Governmental agencies along the Grand Strand and state officials are working on a series of projects totaling about $1 billion to relieve other traffic woes along the beach. Until those new roads are finished, however, visitors and residents alike will continue to be stuck in too many vehicles trying to get the same places at the same time.

Accommodations

Once you've made up your mind to head for the Grand Strand, you've barely started the decision-making process. You first need to decide what kind of beach experience you're looking for, then begin narrowing your choices based on the beaches that meet your preference. If you want a lot to do and a lot of options, Myrtle Beach and the beaches near it will be your target. Otherwise, look to the beaches farther away to the north and south.

In general, the closer you stay to the beach, the higher the room rates. The tariffs are highest in the summer months of June, July, and August—duh—because that's when most people come to the beach. It should come as no surprise to know that many businesses in the area make most of their money each year during the short three-month summer season. Spring and fall are becoming more popular times for visitors; rates are lower then. During the winter months there are many price bargains, even at the most expensive lodgings. Some accommodations are not available for daily rentals, however, especially during the summer months. At Pawleys Island, for instance, beachfront rentals go by the week, and you won't find overnight lodging except at motels along major thoroughfares like US 17.

If your idea of fun is an upscale beachfront hotel, perhaps a high-rise or condo, with restaurants, pools, room service, fitness centers, spas, and such accoutrements, there are plenty along the Grand Strand. Expect to visit the $200 level in peak season (summer) at places like the Sheraton Myrtle Beach or the attractive Embassy Suites at Kingston Plantation, though special packages are frequently available, and the rates drop substantially in the off-season.

A huge variety of accommodations at a slightly lower level of scale exist up and down the Strand. These hotels, motels, condos, inns, and resorts offer pools, rooms or suites, workout rooms, and restaurants (onsite or close by). Rates for beachfront locations in summer go from $125 per night up—and up.

Smaller motels, hotels, and inns with a beachfront location, or perhaps second row, offer summer rates all over the map, from $85 or so nightly upward depending on room size and amenities. For the price, don't expect room service and a robe in the closet.

Farther away from the beach—but still within walking distance to the ocean—visitors may luck into a rate as low as $39. But don't waste too much of your time searching that out. And don't press your fortune by expecting such a bargain on the July Fourth holiday weekend.

There are many chain hotels and motels scattered throughout the Strand, a good number of them far enough away from the beach to require a car to get you there and back. But a lot of vacationers who stay here aren't always looking for the beach. They may be in the market for shopping or entertainment, and the malls, boutiques, and entertainment complexes are almost all found blocks or even miles away from the beachfront. Rates at these lodgings are most often over $100 per night, and they offer the usual conveniences. In the off-season, look for cheaper packages, especially if you're a golfer.

There's scarcely an establishment along the Strand that doesn't have at least a couple of special packages of particular interest to golfers. The rates generally include some arrangement of lodging, food, eighteen or thirty-six

Accommodations on the Grand Strand range from small family-owned motels to national chains to full-scale resorts—some 40,000 rooms in all. (Courtesy Myrtle Beach Area Chamber of Commerce)

holes, a cart, and greens fees. You can find these packages year-round, too. Some of them, in fact, include reduced-rate airfares into Myrtle Beach.

Families who come to the beach to park their recreational vehicle are in luck. The area bills itself, immodestly but not necessarily inaccurately, as "the camping capital of the world." There are more than 7,000 sites between North Myrtle Beach and the south end of Myrtle Beach. There are spots for RVs and tent campers. And you don't even have to have your own RV; you can rent one and use it as your home base during your vacation. The commercial camping areas, by the way, are not exactly rustic. Besides beachfront access, many of them offer pools (even covered pools!), shopping centers, amusement areas, and clubhouses with saunas and fitness centers. Camping at the state parks is a little more primitive and isolated.

Private homes are available for visitors up and down the Grand Strand. Nearly all must be rented for a weekend, two- or three-night minimum stay, or by the week. Rates range from a minimum of several hundred dollars per night to several thousand for a week depending on the amenities and location.

At Pawleys Island, there are a couple of historic lodgings still receiving guests and serving meals. Sea View Inn and Pelican Inn have long been favorites for visitors and offer facilities that reflect an earlier, more genteel era of beachgoing.

Veteran vacationers along the Strand make their reservations early, sometimes a year in advance. If you want very specific accommodations at certain times of the summer, plan on calling early to get them. Six months is not too early. The same advice applies if you want to be on the beach at a very popular time, say July Fourth or the Labor Day weekend. Except for the summer months, such early-bird calls usually are not necessary. And because there are so many places to stay on the Strand, there's hardly any time when you can't just show up at the last minute and find a room (but don't count on it being directly in front of the ocean).

Finally, a couple of tips to remember about accommodations at the Strand:

A few, mostly smaller, properties close up in the winter months, but not nearly as many as a few years ago because Myrtle Beach and environs now offer so many attractions regardless of the season. But if you have a favorite off-the-beaten-path lodging, check with them before assuming they'll be open in January.

Nomenclature is important in determining rates. If an establishment advertises beachfront or oceanfront rooms, that means you should expect to be facing the Atlantic, maybe with a short, straight walk to the beach. "Oceanview" means just that and no more: you have a view of the beach from your room (it can, however, be a tiny view around the corner of a balcony, so don't automatically assume it's a picture postcard view out your front window. Ask before you pay.) "Poolside" or "streetside" tells you where your room faces, which may or may not be to your preference. Regardless, "beachfront" will always cost you more than "oceanview" and anything else.

Traveling with Fido and Fluffy? Be sure to check about pet accommodations when you call or e-mail for a reservation. There aren't many hotels and motels that do accept pets in the Grand Strand. If you're renting a house, you'll want to inquire into the policies for animals also. And remember to keep your pet leashed so as not to inconvenience others and run afoul of city ordinances.

Dining Out

From Little River down to Georgetown, you'll find close to 2,000 restaurants of one sort or another, from seafood palaces to hole-in-the-wall snack bars along with every chain food establishment known to western civilization. You scoff, eh? Driving through the North Myrtle Beach area could make a believer out of you in no time. It is claimed that the Strand offers more dining options per capita than San Francisco. Whether or not that's true, it is a fact that you'll surely find more seafood restaurants here than in any similar stretch in the United States. So don't expect to go hungry during your stay, and don't expect to have to eat seafood if that's your preference. You ought to sample the fresh catches along the beaches, but if you prefer steaks or veggies, you won't have to drive very far. The range of cuisine includes Mexican, Chinese, Japanese, Australian, French, Italian, German, Cajun. Or you can go local and try the sausage grits, lowcountry bog, alligator stew, and the like.

Informality is the rule around the Grand Strand, in the serving of food and the clothes you have to wear while eating it. At bars and stands along the beach, swimsuit attire is not only OK but expected. Generally speaking, elsewhere, you'll need a top of some sort and shoes (and yes, pants, too, though it doesn't matter whether they're short or long). Customers being turned away from restaurants because they don't have a coat and tie are rarer than on-street parking spots in July. Dress up if you wish, but don't think you have to.

Reservations are not necessary here, and there are quite a few restaurants that do not accept them except for large groups. It's always a good idea to check before heading out. If you get hungry for dinner before 5:30 P.M. or after 9:30 P.M. you shouldn't have to worry about long lines. But a number of restaurants in the area feature early bird specials with discounted prices beginning around 4:30 P.M., and they can be very popular with the locals and visitors alike. During the prime dinner hours, though, be prepared for a wait, maybe for an hour or even longer. Between those hours be prepared to wait, maybe for an hour or even a little longer. The turnover is pretty quick at most Strand restaurants, however, so have a cocktail or do a little people-watching while you wait. Lunch lines aren't nearly as long. Breakfast, as your nutritionist no doubt has mentioned, is the most important meal of the day. Around here it's probably the cheapest meal of the day, too. Seafood restaurants, as a rule, don't open for breakfast, but there are lots of other places which do, most starting service at 6 A.M. for early risers.

Dining out along the Strand doesn't have to be expensive. Most restaurants, in fact, fall into the "moderately priced" category. Dinner for two usually ranges from $25 to $40 at full-service restaurants (that doesn't include drinks or tips). Of course you can eat on the cheap almost anywhere. And if you wish, you could spend a lot more, too, though this area doesn't have many high-end establishments. Lunch tabs average perhaps one-third to one-half as much as dinner. Service is casual and usually quick; the kitchen and wait staffs know there is always someone else waiting for a seat.

The dining lure for most visitors to the Grand Strand is—no surprise here—seafood. Shrimp. Fish. Oysters. Clams. Scallops. More shrimp. More fish. Fry 'em. Broil 'em. Steam 'em. Whatever you want, the seafood chefs along the Strand can do it for you.

The specialty of the area is Calabash-style seafood, and visitors will see numerous signs along restaurant rows advertising Calabash. Don't be put off or puzzled by them. The explanation is very simple. The name comes from a small fishing village just across the state line in North Carolina, where this style of cooking started around the 1930s. The seafood is dipped in lightly seasoned batter and served golden brown and very hot. It usually comes with French fries or baked potato, cole slaw, or salad and hush puppies (hot balls of batter-fried cornmeal). The servings traditionally are generous. The calories invariably are prodigious. But after a day of surf and sun, there are few better-tasting and more satisfying meals. Of course it's possible your nutritionist might conclude otherwise, but then you're the one who's on vacation. Besides, envy is not a pretty thing.

The turnover of restaurants makes specific listings out of date almost as quickly as they appear. Ask at your hotel or motel or pick up one of the many free newspaper and magazine listings that proliferate at street corners and in front of lodgings around the Strand. There are, however, several restaurants that have been around for so long they have acquired a certain aura, and visitors may want to check them out for historical as well as appetite-appeasing reasons. For instance, the Sea Captain's House in the middle of Myrtle Beach (3002 N. Ocean Blvd.) has been serving up seafood from its famous ocean-front location for nearly forty years. And Oliver's Lodge in Murrells Inlet has been operating even a bit longer; several generations have put away shrimp and scallops here. These establishments are landmarks of the Grand Strand, having survived time, hurricanes, and the fickleness of public taste. They are well worth noting in an area where change—by intent or nature—long has been a way of life.

Shopping

It's hard to resist the siren call to buy when there are so many retail establishments crying out. They line the roads, they fill the shopping centers, they beckon alluringly with treasures big and small, expensive and low-priced. They are one of the four reasons visitors come to the Strand (the others are the beach, golf, and entertainment). And should you happen to need a beach towel, you may get dizzy before settling on just one of the multitudes of shops selling towels and other beach-related paraphernalia. (Take a spin on US 17 north or south of Myrtle Beach to see the evidence of this astonishing proliferation.) Most stores are open seven days a week, though Sunday hours may be abbreviated.

If you forgot to bring something from home, fear not; there's a place— probably at least hundreds of them—where you can replace it easily. The Strand as a rule offers a plethora of moderately priced shops of all goods. There are a few higher-end stores and lots more with inexpensive stock. Your biggest decision likely will be where to start.

Starting at the top, don't go looking for Neiman Marcus and Louis Vuitton. This is the Grand Strand, not Rodeo Drive. On the other hand, there are a bunch of recognizable names represented here: Coach, Laura Ashley, Eddie Bauer, Polo, Geoffrey Beene, Tommy Hilfiger, J. Crew, London Fog, Lenox, Movado, Victoria's Secret, and their ilk. The outlets and department stores such as Wal-Mart, K-Mart, Target, Sears, and Belk abound through the Strand's sixty miles. And there is a wealth of smaller independents and chains selling everything from hammocks to perfume, sofas to model trains.

There are several major, easy-to-find shopping "communities" where most of the crowds congregate. Broadway at the Beach (off the 17 Bypass) is so remarkable it won an award in 1996 as South Carolina's top tourist attraction. It's a center for not only shopping but restaurants and nightlife as well. There are more than eighty stores set around a man-made freshwater lake with themed areas carrying shoppers from the Caribbean to a New England fishing village.

Barefoot Landing (US 17 North) is another complex of shops, dining, and entertainment. Unusually attractive and built around—rather than burying—the natural environment, it features dozens of eclectic stores around a waterway that is home to alligators, seagulls, turtles, fish, and a variety of aquatic creatures, all easily glimpsed. Also on the north end of the Strand are Briarcliffe Mall and Myrtle Square Mall, while to the south are Inlet Square Mall at Murrells Inlet and the Hammock Shop at Pawleys Island. The latter has been around since the 1930s, though it is now much expanded into a conclave of dozens of little shops selling much more than hammocks.

On US 501 between Myrtle Beach and Conway—but closest to Myrtle Beach—is the Outlet Park at Waccamaw anchored by Waccamaw Pottery, the Strand's oldest "big" store. It is huge: more than three football fields, selling well, just about anything you need and probably a lot of stuff you never imagined. There are other stores surrounding it, too, so many that a tram is available to carry shoppers around the complex. Look out for buses filled with bargain-hunters pulling up in the parking lot.

Just a couple of miles away (in the direction of Conway) is Myrtle Beach Factory Stores, a large outlet park with some of the better-known brand-name stores represented and goods selling at discount.

And there's another store that deserves mention, if for no reason other than its presence on the beachfront smack in the middle of downtown Myrtle Beach for generations. The Gay Dolphin has been selling beach goods and odds and ends since the 1950s, and its latest reincarnation has tripled its size and stock. You can't miss it whether you're walking or driving Ocean Boulevard or strolling along the beach; it's next door to the pavilion and amusement park.

That hardly exhausts the list of shopping centers—there's a store almost everywhere you look—but it perhaps suggests where the largest concentration of shopping delights exists around the Strand. By the way, there's no shortage of groceries here either, from small convenience stores to mega-groceries like Kroger, Winn-Dixie, Food Lion, and Harris Teeter. There's a location every few blocks, so don't be concerned about running short of provisions.

Golf

Golf has to rate a separate category because it has been a major ingredient in the fuel that drives Myrtle Beach up, and out. For tens of thousands of men and women each year, in fact, golf is the raison d'etre along the Grand Strand. And why not? The courses are beautifully arrayed, there are scads of them, they can be relatively inexpensive, and they can be played every month of the year, a few passing hurricanes and nor'easters notwithstanding. No wonder there were nearly four million individual rounds of golf reported on the Strand a couple of years back.

There are more than 100 courses scattered throughout the Strand, the highest ratio of courses to people anywhere in the nation. The best rank among the best anywhere. And even the least among them has challenges for all but the near-professional-level golfer. The first one was built in Myrtle Beach in 1927—Pine Lakes, and you can still play a round there—but even into the 1960s it had only a little company. That changed quickly, however, and by the late 1990s there were far more golf courses than McDonald's restaurants in the area.

Golf Digest magazine has rated the Strand as the nation's best destination for golfers. The state of South Carolina and the local chamber of commerce officials market golf facilities aggressively, and this has meant lots of special incentives to golfers around the nation. Nearly every hotel, motel, and resort worth its name has at least one golf package with reduced rates for accommodations, meals, and greens fees to lure golfers to the area. The packages are especially low during the summer and winter months, when you can play a weekend of golf and get a couple of nights at a motel for not much more than the greens fees at some other areas. It's possible to arrive at the Strand, go directly to the course, play eighteen holes, and have a meal before checking in at your hotel. And you can spend the next week playing thirty-six holes a day at different courses up and down the Strand, if that's your desire. All but a handful of the courses are open to the public through some sort of package; inquire at your hotel or through the chamber of commerce.

A number of national men's and women's tournaments have been played over Strand courses, including the Senior Tour Championship and the DuPont

With capacity for 3 million rounds of golf annually, the Myrtle Beach
area is America's second most popular golfing destination, after Florida.
(Courtesy Myrtle Beach Area Chamber of Commerce)

World Amateur Handicap Championship. Some of the courses have been designed by the well-known likes of Jack Nicklaus, Rees Jones, Gary Player, Raymond Floyd, Pete Dye, Robert Trent Jones, and Arnold Palmer. The layouts follow the natural landscape around lovely marshlands, river bluffs, towering oak trees, and spectacular vistas. The Dunes Golf and Beach Club in North Myrtle Beach is perhaps the best known, a Robert Trent Jones-designed course, one of the oldest on the Strand and long regarded among the finest in America. Its legendary (and treacherous) thirteenth has been chosen among the "100 Best Holes in America" by *Southern Living* magazine. Among other highly acclaimed courses are The Legends, Myrtle Beach National, Wild Wing Plantation, and River Oaks Gold Plantation, though that only skirts the listing of the myriad of enjoyable links from Little River to Pawleys.

"Teed off" in this part of the country means only that you've started playing your round.

Entertainment/Nightlife

You can, of course, sit in your room and watch television. And you can escape the heat and get caught up on your reading at the public libraries in the area. But when the sun goes down and the lights come on, nearly everyone who comes to Myrtle Beach goes out for something, whether it's to a club, to see a big-name entertainer, to hit the malls, or to check out a show. Myrtle Beach was invented for going out. There are all kinds of places to go and things to do along the Strand, but the nighttime pulse beats strongest when you arrive in Myrtle Beach.

It's a good idea to understand the rules before you get started, and South Carolina has some . . . well, unusual liquor laws. The legal age to imbibe liquor, beer, or wine is twenty-one. It's strictly enforced. Be prepared to show a photo identification card (such as driver's license) if you even look like you might be under the legal age. Some clerks have been known to ask even some women of a certain age to show an ID just as a friendly gesture. But no matter where you buy your alcoholic beverages—nightclub, liquor store, or party shop— you will be asked for an ID. And beware of driving after drinking; the police will check and they will arrest.

If you want to buy a bottle of liquor in South Carolina, look for a store with a red dot on the side. There are plenty of them at the beaches, and by law they can sell only between the hours of 9 A.M. and 7 P.M. (Their closing hours used to be sunset, but since that varied so wildly with the time of year and daylight savings time, would-be purchasers could find stores closing almost by midafternoon in the winter months. The howl of consumers was heard in the state capitol, and legislators voted to make the change several decades ago.)

Party shops or convenience stores with a license may sell beer and wine for longer hours. Nearly all clubs and restaurants at the beaches sell alcoholic beverages seven days a week. State law requires that liquor served in clubs and restaurants be dispensed by mini-bottles, which hold 1.6 ounces. Your server is supposed to bring the bottle to your table and open it in your presence, but that hardly ever happens. You'll get a drink just as you order it and probably will never see the mini-bottle from which it came. Just another one of South Carolina's liquor law peculiarities.

Another peculiarity is has to do with the state's so-called "blue laws," which prohibit the sale of certain items on Sundays in some parts of the state. The law was passed many years ago when lawmakers felt that selling goods on Sunday might be a lure to keep some people away from church. In recent years, beach counties, tourist destinations, and the state's larger metropolitan areas have exempted themselves. As a result, visitors will find some stores open on Sunday mornings while many others, particularly those in malls, don't open until the early afternoon. It can be a bit confusing; ask at your hotel or motel for up-to-the-minute clarification.

Of course there are lots of things to do that don't require an ID. Miniature golf, for example. The miniature golf courses offer eighteen or thirty-six holes at locations from Little River to Pawleys for which you don't need a cart. But you do need some putting skills to overcome the amazing obstacles that course designers have set up—everything from roaring dinosaurs to raging waterfalls. The hazards are the fun, of course, and all ages can play and enjoy themselves. Tasteful is not always the operative word for these roadside enterprises, so drive on by if you wish. But be prepared for the kids to yell, "I wanna stop."

Myrtle Beach has a new minor league baseball team, a Class A affiliate of the Atlanta Braves. The team plays its home games at night from April through August at a comfy new $12 million stadium adjacent to Broadway at the Beach.

Naturally there are plenty of options for water-related fun. How about renting a boat? Pontoon, jet ski, kayak, canoe, motorboat, sailing vessel—you name it, if it moves on the water, you can rent it on the Strand. You can also rent scuba equipment, try parasailing, or go windsurfing. You can charter a boat for deep-sea fishing expeditions, or take a leisurely cruise along the Waccamaw River and see some of the old rice plantations that used to generate the wealth in this region before the tourists arrived. Heck, you can even go swimming in the ocean. At the state parks, you can head out on a nature trail to get an appreciation of the coastal region's natural environment. Water, after all, is why Myrtle Beach got started—even before the first golf course was built.

By the way, outdoor-lovers whose passion is tennis haven't been neglected in the area. There are more than 200 courts, many of them lighted, for play up and down the Strand. Some are connected to hotels or resorts, others are public. Fees are usually very reasonable, and they are open year-round.

Mammoth entertainment complexes—blocks and in some cases miles from the beachfront—have sprung up around Myrtle Beach in recent years, and they are huge lures for visitors in pursuit of sundown fun. The pubs and clubs have live entertainment just about every night in summer and on weekends the rest of the year. Broadway at the Beach seems to be the busiest complex and features the entertainment area known as Celebrity Square. There is a nominal charge at some of the clubs in the area, which offer music from Top 40s to shag to blues. Some have a bit of a bawdy atmosphere, others are a little more laid back. No matter, the noise and fun levels can get pretty high. At

A moving sidewalk takes visitors through Ripley's Aquarium, one of the many attractions at the Broadway at the Beach complex. (Courtesy Myrtle Beach Area Chamber of Commerce)

the end of Celebrity Square is the entrance to the popular pyramid-shaped Hard Rock Café and not far away is Planet Hollywood.

Broadway at the Beach is also the home of an IMAX theater with its super sound and six-story-high movie screen. There are shows every day and evening. Also nearby is Ripley's Aquarium, a $37 million attraction that is both informative and entertaining. Since it's built by the folks who brought you "Ripley's Believe It or Not," sort of an off-the-wall freak museum, you might wonder whether it's really a legitimate attraction. The answer is yes, it most definitely is. The packaging is entertaining and fun-oriented, certainly, but the lessons are educational as well for kids and their grown-ups.

New to Broadway at the Beach is the Butterfly Pavilion, a $7.5 million facility which houses a forty-foot high butterfly conservatory and restaurant.

Dinner theaters have found a home in Myrtle Beach. There are two of them: Medieval Times and the Dixie Stampede. Both might be considered corny by some folks, maybe, but the growing crowds suggest they are very appealing for many others. Medieval Times (near Waccamaw Pottery off US 501) is set inside a castle where audiences on opposite sides lustily cheer on their favorites in a lively jousting competition (complete with real horses and occasional spills) while dining on a hearty meal. At the Dixie Stampede (where US 17 Bypass meets US 17 in North Myrtle Beach), the theme is country rodeo with horseback riding, gun-shooting, and some nifty acts based on the seasons, including a special Christmas show. A big meal is served, and audiences are encouraged to yell for their favorites.

The growth of theaters in the Myrtle Beach area in the 1990s has brought an influx of entertainment to the area unmatched in its history. The theaters have been the catalyst for a flood of tourists looking for some beach fun and a little shopping topped off by an evening with performers like Donny and Marie Osmond, Tom Jones, Dolly Parton, the cast of *Cats,* Clint Black, B. B. King, Sheena Easton, Kenny Rogers, Aretha Franklin, *Riverdance,* Connie Francis, Harry Belafonte, Jim Nabors, Lily Tomlin, and Travis Tritt.

Among the other large theaters are the Carolina Opry—which hosts not just country music but Broadway shows and pop artists as well—and the Crook and Chase Theater, where the Nashville Network's Crook and Chase television show is taped part of the year. (Note: Some of these establishments are subject to waves of popularity, and when the tide is out, they may be closed or being renovated for new ownership.)

One of the most popular stops for young people is the House of Blues, which draws regional and national rock and pop acts for concerts year-round. In addition, its gospel brunch from 9 A.M. to 2 P.M. every Sunday is a popular stop for adults as well. The cost is $16.95, which includes all the gospel music you want.

Advance reservations are necessary for the theater complexes, especially in summer but hardly less so at other times of year since Myrtle Beach is becoming a year-round destination. In fact, if you're thinking about a Saturday night show June through August, it's a good idea to call ahead for reservations before you get to the beach. The theaters can handle large groups easily, but it's essential they have as much notice as possible. For the biggest acts, advance tickets are a must.

Clubs and pubs don't take reservations; they assume folks will walk up whenever they're interested. If one is crowded, don't go far away; chances are the turnover will create some space within a few minutes. But do be careful about driving away after having a few alcoholic beverages.

Before the advent of theaters, Myrtle Beach used to be famous for its amusement park downtown at the beachfront. The Pavilion Amusement Park was the center of nightlife for the entire Grand Strand. Teens would meet their dates, or cruise the area hoping to meet the opposite sex. Kiddies would scream with joy at the rides. Adults would settle for conversation and that all-time favorite activity, people-watching.

There was a time, back in the late 1980s and early '90s, when this area looked run-down. But the amusement park has been the scene of renovation costing millions of dollars aimed at restoring it to a prime place in the hearts of beach-goers. Its 11 acres now include a host of fun and thrill rides for all ages, and there's an alcohol-free club for teens at the Pavilion. Parking can be a problem when things are going full blast, but walking around is the way this area was meant to be enjoyed.

Water parks are scattered around the Grand Strand. They are where you go when you want to get wet, which might seem a bit odd given that the Atlantic Ocean isn't very far away. But there seems to be special fun in getting wet in other places. There are at least three parks in operation during the summer, one in North Myrtle Beach on the 17 Bypass, another in Myrtle Beach's Ocean Boulevard, and a third at Surfside Beach. Also, fans of stock car racing won't want to miss a stop at the NASCAR Café to share a meal with mementos of their favorite drivers, and nearby are go-karts waiting for a spin around the mini-track.

For More Information

The Greater Myrtle Beach Chamber of Commerce has all sorts of information about the Grand Strand, including telephone numbers and addresses for anything and everything you might need. It's fully staffed every day and ready to help.

FOR INFORMATION call the Greater Myrtle Beach Chamber of Commerce at 800) 356-3016 or (843) 626-7444, or go to www.myrtlebeachlive.com. They'll be glad to send information about lodgings, restaurants, attractions, shopping, and everything else referred to in this section of the book Also, the South Carolina Department of Parks, Recreation and Tourism also has lots of material to help plan a trip. Call (803) 734-1700 or visit their website, www.travelsc.com.

Two

The Grand Strand

South

FOR INFORMATION on weather, driving directions, restaurants, accommodations, and other details about locations throughout the Grand Strand, see pages 12–27.

Surfside Beach

The south portion of the Grand Strand begins with Surfside Beach just to the south of the Myrtle Beach city limits. The frantic pace of Myrtle Beach begins to slow in these beaches, reaching something of an apex at Pawleys Island a little father south. Along US 17, there is the usual profusion of beachwear shops and restaurants and traffic. But once a visitor heads over to the beach, the scene gets a little quieter, the buildings a lot smaller and the entertainment choices considerably more limited—at least when compared to Myrtle Beach. The pier is a target for kids looking for a little action and grown-ups eager to try their luck fishing. Surfside and the beaches continuing to the south draw groups and families looking for somewhat less frenetic surroundings.

Garden City

Garden City has an even more residential feel to it and offers a number of cottages, smaller houses, and accommodations for visitors who want to be a little bit farther away from the bright lights of Myrtle Beach. Fishing off the pier, or just sitting and sunning on this structure jutting into the ocean is a popular activity in all but the very coldest of weather. Nearby restaurants make this a popular stopping point for hungry travelers, too.

Murrells Inlet

Murrells Inlet is the oldest fishing village along the Grand Strand, a quiet community—and incidentally, the longtime home of master mystery writer Mickey Spillane (*I, the Jury*)—that doesn't draw visitors looking for beaches. This is instead a place for fishing charters, kicking back a little, and—to be blunt about it—eating. There are several cottages and small motels, but it's decidedly more residential in nature than just about everywhere else along the Strand. It suffered a big hit from Hurricane Hugo in 1989, but it came back with new housing and new resolve. Fishing and crabbing in the creeks and marshes is fun, and so is heading out for a deep-sea trip to catch the big ones. There are boats which can haul you to the feeding grounds of the most exciting deep-sea fishes, but there are also more sedate journeys up and down the waterways (the sunset cruises are especially popular) that offer educational and fun looks at the history and lifestyles of the coast.

For landlubbers, Murrells Inlet is famous for its seafood restaurants arrayed along what is locally called "The Seafood Mile." It seems as if there must be one for at least every year-round resident of the town. Don't think, however, that because of that you won't find a crowd. In the summer and even on out-of-busy-season weekends, the restaurants will be jammed starting as early as 5 P.M., so be prepared to wait. The reason is simple: the food is good, and the catch is fresh, plentiful and not expensive. The restaurants have a lot of atmosphere, many of them with views into the picturesque marsh, and the fish and shellfish can be as fresh as the haul from today's shrimpers. Name your seafood favorite and you'll find it in abundance here.

Huntington Beach State Park

FOR INFORMATION call the state park at (843) 237-4440 or go to www.southcarolinaparks.com.
••

The second state park within the Grand Strand, Huntington Beach is three miles south of Murrells Inlet, directly across US 17 from the entrance to Brookgreen Gardens.

The famous Gardens deserve a special mention, although they are not a park of the state park system. They are home to a world-class collection of outdoor statuary, many of the works created by the late Anna Hyatt Huntington but also including works by such American artists as Marshall Fredericks, Daniel Chester French, Gutzon Borglum, Frederic Remington, and Carl Milles. Brookgreen is the world's largest outdoor sculpture garden, and many of the works here in their beautiful natural setting will take your breath away. It's best to allot at least half a day to savor the experience at Brookgreen. There is an admission charge, and visitors will find food and drink available on the grounds.

There's a long and rich history associated with this land, which was home to some of the most successful rice plantations and wealthiest plantation owners in the mid-nineteenth century. The value of the property declined precipitously after the Civil War and into the twentieth century. Anna Huntington and her husband Archer bought it in 1929, and soon thereafter began the creation of this magnificent attraction.

The *Fighting Stallions* sculpture, completed when Anna was seventy-five, was placed by the highway in 1951 to draw the attention of passing motorists. Now it has become the symbol for Brookgreen and helps to lure thousands of visitors each year. There are driving and walking areas in the Gardens and several separate museums along with a Botanical Garden, a walk-through aviary and a fifty-acre wildlife park (the kids especially will get a kick out of the animals, most of them, native to the Palmetto State). Brookgreen has guided walking tours available and also offers 45-minute tours around the old rice fields on a pontoon boat. Don't get there too late, however; the boat tours are offered only at 11 A.M. and 1, 2, and 3 P.M. daily, weather permitting. If you're visiting in the summer, know it will be very hot and humid and buggy. Dress accordingly with a hat and be sure to bring along water and some insect repellent. To help ease the heat, there are some special evening hours during the summer.

FOR INFORMATION on Brookgreen Gardens, call (843) 237-4218 or visit www.brookgreen.com.

••

After you've seen Brookgreen, drive across the road—look carefully, this is a very busy highway in the summer months—and you'll see the entrance to Huntington Beach State Park, named for the sculptor who gave her name to this gorgeous 2,500-acre facility which sits in a stunning natural environment. There's a small admission fee to get in, and the ranger who collects it will give visitors a brochure directing them around the grounds. Take your time; there's a lot to see and enjoy, and it's all free once you've paid the fee (which helps provide for the upkeep of the parks throughout South Carolina).

Atalaya, home of Anna Hyatt Huntington, is open for tours in the summer and for other events throughout the year. (Courtesy Myrtle Beach Area Chamber of Commerce)

The Mullet Pond on the right soon after you enter is home to a large number of alligators, which do not care much for intruders. This is one place to avoid stepping into, and there are no nearby parking places—for good reason. To the left, the tidal salt marsh is home to many species of birds—nearly 300 can be found around the park, which is regarded as among the top birding sites along the East Coast—and there's a handicapped-accessible boardwalk with a fifty-foot observation deck where varieties of birdlife can be viewed easily.

Of course there's the beach, too, and it's beautiful, wide, and often surprisingly uncrowded. There are bathhouse facilities. Fishing is welcome in the surf or along the jetty. The park office even has tackle for use if you've forgotten your equipment.

Anna Huntington's Moorish castlelike winter home, Atalaya, is where some of her works were created. The outrageously romantic old house, with its many rooms and spacious courtyard in a spectacular outdoor setting, is eagerly sought after by visitors planning weddings or other social gatherings within its walls. There are interior tours scheduled daily in summer, and in September of each year, Atalaya hosts a nationally acclaimed juried arts and crafts festival.

For most people, Huntington Beach is a day-use state park. The lucky ones who can lay early claim to one of the 127 sites for tents or RVs, however, can enjoy its beauty and solitude overnight. Once again, it's hard to believe

Huntington Beach State Park, one of several beachfront parks in the South Carolina state park system, offers spaces for tent and RV camping. (Courtesy South Carolina Department of Parks, Recreation & Tourism)

such an oasis of peace can be found amid the crush of humanity at so many other points up and down the Grand Strand.

Litchfield Beach

FOR INFORMATION about Litchfield, call one of the beach rental companies at (888) 714-5993, (800) 476-2861, or (800) 937-7352.

North Litchfield Beach and Litchfield were developed beginning in the 1950s and take their name from an old rice plantation on the nearby Waccamaw River. The moss-draped surroundings, the absence of neon, the smallness of scale, and the presence of residences here appropriately evoke a less hectic pace than that of some of the busier beaches to the north.

Take just a moment first to understand the geography of Litchfield. North Litchfield and Litchfield are public beaches separated by the privately owned Litchfield Beach and Golf Resort. You can walk on the beach from North Litchfield to Litchfield, but you can't drive between them on the road that runs closest and parallel to beachfront homes. To get from one to the other, you have to go back to US 17 and drive a couple of miles past the Beach and Golf Resort, then follow the signs to the appropriate beach. It's a little unwieldy if you're going from North Litchfield to Litchfield, but in fact most people who are staying at one beach seem to have little reason to drive to the other.

The accommodations at Litchfield range from private homes to condos to villas to high-rise apartments to private hotel/resorts. Homes go for up to $2,500 per week in summer, and villas range from about $1,100 to $1,800 per week.

At the Litchfield Beach and Golf Resort, which has facilities to take care of conference groups, beachfront condos go for upwards of $280 per night for a two-bedroom unit, while golf-side two-bedroom villas are around $200 in high season. Off-season rates can drop by as much as two-thirds. There are golf packages available, priced lower in the hot summer months than in the more temperate spring and fall.

The Litchfield Inn, located at Litchfield Beach, is one of the vintage properties in the area with oceanfront rooms ranging from efficiencies to two-bedroom units. Midsummer rates average between $110 and $200 depending on specific times and locations. Specially priced golf packages also are offered year-round; the highest rates are in the spring and fall.

Litchfield Plantation is a country inn on the Waccamaw River (not on the beach) which has four grand suites, a guesthouse with six bedrooms, and several cottages. Guests may enjoy a private marina, dining facilities, and access to tennis and golf.

The clean, sandy beaches are the focal point of entertainment for many visitors to the Litchfield area, but guests at the Beach and Golf Resort also have access to a health club with sauna and fitness programs, summer adventure camps for kids, indoor and outdoor pools, a tennis club, and three golf courses.

As it is everywhere along the Grand Strand, golf is what brings thousands to the coast annually. In the Litchfield area, there are more than a dozen eighteen-hole courses to test even the finest golfers. Among them:

- Litchfield Country Club, par 72, 6,752 yards, with driving range, practice green, lounge, pro shop
- Blackmoor, par 72, 6,614 yards with driving range, pro shop, practice green.
- Wachesaw Plantation East, par 72, 6,618 yards, with driving range, putting greens, pro shop, snack bar
- River Club, par 72, 6,677 yards with practice green, snack bar, pro shop
- Willbrook Plantation, par 72, 6,704 yards, home of the Bryan Van Der Riet Golf Academy, with complete facilities

- Tradition Club, par 72, 6,919 yards with 43,000-square foot putting green, snack bar, lounge, pro shop

Carts are required at all courses. All offer play along beautiful, mossy tidal marshes, not oceanfront layouts.

Shoppers will find a modest number of shopping outlets in Litchfield. For greater variety, head north on US 17 in the southern end of Myrtle Beach where stores and shops and malls line both sides of the road. Also, there are points along the highway here where visitors can take a boat tour on the Waccamaw River. The easygoing tours allow the viewing of historic lands and commentary on the history of the South Carolina lowcountry.

Pawleys Island

FOR INFORMATION about Pawleys, contact the Georgetown County Chamber of Commerce, Box 1776, Georgetown, SC 29440, or call (800) 777-7705. For rental information, contact Pawleys Island Realty Company, (800) 937-7352 or (843) 237-4257, or Smith Real Estate, (800) 476-5651.

• •

Four miles long and barely a quarter of a mile wide, reached by two causeways off US 17, Pawleys Island has a rich and fascinating history that goes back to the early 1800s. It also comes with its own unique ghost, the "Gray Man" of widespread legend, whose origins vary from storyteller to storyteller but whose appearance has come to be a welcome herald for approaching severe storms.

(Doubters should know that this writer can claim a sighting back in the 1950s, when the mysterious figure of a man cloaked in gray was glimpsed on a faraway dune shortly before a terrible storm lashed the beach. The storm caused substantial damage to homes and inns but no loss of life, thanks to those who heeded the ghost's warning to get inside. Scoff if you wish, but . . .)

There's an undeniable romance about Pawleys, located three miles south of Litchfield Beach. Part of that stems from its history—it was a summer resort for wealthy plantation owners of the South Carolina lowcountry and has always possessed a certain cachet—and in part from its determination to remain far away from the lights and hurly-burly activity of Myrtle Beach. Residents and longtime visitors have long proudly shown off bumper stickers which advertise Pawleys as "Arrogantly Shabby," and they have used that designation to reflect a way of life here.

(The *WPA Guide to the Palmetto State*, published in 1941, had this observation about Pawleys: "The casual dress of Pawley's Island's summer residents astonishes newcomers. Bare feet are the rule, even for bank presidents; girls

A Pawleys Island hammock is the perfect spot to relax—no matter where you are on the South Carolina coast. (Photograph by William W. Starr)

dance at the Pavilion in sweeping evening gowns but without any shoes or stockings.")

The oldest houses, inns, and cottages have retained a weathered, rustic look by intent as well as response to nature's whims. Some are so covered by overgrowth they have all but disappeared from the two-lane road that parallels the beach. Pawleys, therefore, carries a bit of a reclusive feel to it along with the sense of old and established.

Hurricane Hugo in 1989 caused substantial rearrangement at Pawleys; it virtually cut the island in half, and many homes were lost. With a frenzy of building and restoring over the last decade, it can be hard to tell what was lost. Whatever has come its way, Pawleys, most visitors seem to agree, has lost little of its charm and allure.

The accommodations at Pawleys are priced in line with many of the resorts along the coast. The oldest of them tend to rent year after year to the same families at the same time of year, so don't expect to stroll into one of them at the last minute over the Fourth of July weekend. In fact, just about everything on Pawleys rents by the week or more during the summer months. Depending on location—beachfront homes go for more, of course—and the size of the house, summer rentals at Pawleys can top $3,000. Don't expect much lower than $1,000 per week in summer for anything. (During the winter months, there are a number of homes available for rental by the week or month, and the rates drop off by more than half.)

Along US 17 at Pawleys are several lodgings—including Hampton Inn, Ramada and Pawleys Plantation (villas)—that specialize in golf packages for adjacent courses. The nightly prices generally range between $75 and $125 in the spring and fall, about one-third less at other times.

The eighteen-hole courses in the vicinity are beautifully landscaped and feature play amidst towering live oaks, historic rice fields, and lovely marshes. They include:

- Caledonia, par 70, 6,526 yards with hitting area, practice green, restaurant, and pro shop
- Sea Gull, par 72, 6,910 yards, practice green, grill, pro shop
- True Blue (opened 1998), par 72, 7,010 yards with driving range, putting green, snack bar, lounge, and pro shop
- Pawleys Plantation (designed by Jack Nicklaus), par 72, 7,026 yards with Phil Ritson–Mel Sole Golf School, complete practice facilities, restaurant, pro shop; also swimming pool, tennis courts.

Apart from golf, fun at Pawleys is considerably more subdued and infinitely less crowded than "up nawth" (as longtime visitors of Pawleys are inclined to refer to Myrtle Beach). Surf fishing is popular and occasionally produces some spectacular catches. And so is crabbing, which requires patience and quietness, attributes that seem perfectly attuned to this beach. Beachcombing, sitting on screened-in porches, and just cooling it is about as good as it gets here and as it has been for darned near two centuries. Relaxing is a way of life at Pawleys. Even the charming little nondenominational church in the middle of the island has glass windows enabling Sunday worshipers to view the serenity of the marsh.

Relaxing is so famous around here that the islanders have created their own hammock, a name well known around the world. A Pawleys Island rope hammock is a treat for all ages; try one and see how long you can last before dozing off. This type of hammock is said to have been invented by Joshua Ward of nearby Brookgreen Plantation in the early nineteenth century and later duplicated and marketed very successfully. It's a cool and comfortable way of letting go. You can purchase one at the Hammock Shop on US 17 at Pawleys, where you can also see them being made. The Hammock Shop has been a famous landmark for several generations and recently added a number of adjoining stores selling everything from jewelry to Christmas decorations.

The complex also has several restaurants (Tyler's Cove has a welcoming fireplace for winter dining) and other appealing little boutiques.

There are several other restaurants in this area along US 17; the best-known and the best, in the minds of many Pawleys residents and visitors, is Frank's. It opened just over a dozen years ago and has been serving up a delightfully eclectic mix of dining experiences ever since. Sure, there's good, fresh seafood here, but the chef has lots of surprises, from Southwestern cuisine to Asian fusion. There's also a good wine list. And in the same gourmet complex is another restaurant, Out Back, which features luncheon specialties (Frank's is open only for dinner) along with a shop packed with cheeses, wines, and other items you might not expect to find at a beach locale. Frank's is very popular; be sure to make a reservation.

If you've got the kids along and they're hollering for a Happy Meal, be assured there are several of the chain fast-food restaurants on this same strip of highway.

And while you're at Pawleys, you may want to stop by All Saints Waccamaw Episcopal Church at Pawleys, one of the best-known churches in the South Carolina coastal area. The existing old church is the fourth building at the site and dates from 1917 (a new and much larger church is across the street). The cemetery contains the remains of many famous planters in this area as well as those who did not survive the terrible storm of 1893, which devastated the coast. The old church is open only on special Sundays, but the cemetery grounds are accessible without charge. All Saints Waccamaw is opposite the beach side of US 17 at Pawleys. Turn onto Waverly Road (state road S-22-46) at the traffic light at the North Causeway entrance to Pawleys Island and follow the signs; it's about two miles.

Pawleys obviously has a distinctive personality, which not all of the Grand Strand beaches can claim with such certainty and tradition. Ironically, it's a beach that can feel at once snobbish yet totally public. Anyone can rent here and feel totally at home. And there's a small public parking area at the south end for day-trippers. But when you come to Pawleys, you've got to come on its terms. No one will ever confuse those with Myrtle Beach, even if they are just a few miles apart and a part of the same Grand Strand.

DeBordieu Colony

FOR INFORMATION on DeBordieu, call (800) 797-3633 or (843) 527-9894.

A lot of South Carolinians call it "Debby-do." Residents of this private, gated beach community would prefer you harken back to the French, where the story gets a little tangled but sounds pretty good. According to this version of the tale, the island acquired its name when the Marquis de Lafayette arrived from France in 1777 during the American Revolution, putting ashore somewhere in the neighborhood. When he saw the beautiful land, he is alleged to have declared it must be "the borderland of God" (*d'abord Dieu*). However, the French doesn't exactly translate back into English as "borderland of God," so perhaps someone misheard the Marquis. Some researchers have suggested the name is simply a corruption of the family name of an early French settler. But then there's also a story about French passengers shipwrecked after a terrible storm. Those who managed to get ashore safely fell on their knees and gave thanks for being saved by the mercy of God, "*de bon Dieu*." Whatever the truth, a lot of people have apparently concurred with the blessings and found this particular piece of land to be quite spectacular, indeed.

DeBordieu celebrates a beautiful six-and-a-half-mile stretch of beach about six miles south of Pawleys Island. It represents the southernmost beach in the Grand Strand and boasts its own eighteen-hole golf course, tennis club, boat ramp, and beach club. Luvan Boulevard splits the island, running from the entrance on US 17, dead-ending at the Beach Club in the middle of the beach. The homes, condos, and villas on the island are a mix of year-round residences and rental units, and all are what could safely be termed upscale.

Villas on the oceanfront, marsh, lagoon, or golf course may be rented weekly (and daily at certain times of year). Weekly rates range from around $1,500 to over $4,000 in summer, a bit less at other times. Location and size of the rental units determine the rates. DeBordieu is a fairly recent development along the coast, going back to the 1980s, so the homes here are of more recent vintage than in some private coastal locations. All come equipped with almost anything a vacationing family could imagine.

Weekly rates for the homes start at close to $2,000 in most cases and go upward to nearly $6,000. Needless to say, renters will not lack for luxury. Nor will they want for things to do. There's the beach, of course, with plenty of access lanes for those who are staying off the ocean. The Beach Club has dining and lounge facilities for guests at DeBordieu, and there are nearby spots for good fishing and crabbing.

The golf course is for the use of guests only, making tee times easy to pick up even at the last minute. The par 72 Pete and P. B. Dye–designed links offer panoramic views for golfers and enough challenges for the best. There's also a lovely clubhouse with complete facilities. Tennis buffs can work out on eight clay courts, several with lights. Lessons in golf and tennis are available for all ages.

Just a few hundred yards south of the entrance to DeBordieu on US 17 is Hobcaw Barony Visitor Center. This area, once home to as many as eleven prosperous rice plantations, was acquired by a well-off stockbroker from New York named Bernard Baruch between 1905 and 1907. Baruch, a South Carolina native and later an adviser to American presidents from Woodrow Wilson to John F. Kennedy, spent much time here and entertained some of the world's most famous leaders at his estate (Winston Churchill and Franklin D. Roosevelt among them). The land is now given over to research in forestry and marine biology by the University of South Carolina and Clemson University. The visitor center is the starting point for tours, which allow access to the Baruch estate, Hobcaw Barony. Admission to the center is free; it is open weekdays and on Saturdays June through August. Advance reservations are necessary for a tour of the Baruch estate, for which a fee is charged. Those tours are offered at 10 A.M. Tuesdays, Wednesdays and Thursdays.

FOR INFORMATION about Hobcaw, call (843) 546-4623.

Vacationers looking for any more action will have to head up the coast in the direction of Myrtle Beach, thirty-five miles away, or to Georgetown three miles to the south. Most DeBordieu visitors, however, seem perhaps understandably content to stay pretty much where they are.

South Carolina

Georgetown

17

McClellanville

17

Francis
Marion
National
Forest

Lake
Moultrie

Cooper River

17

26

Isle of Palms

Sullivan's Island

Charleston

Folly Beach

17

Kiawah Island

Seabrook Island

95

Edisto Beach

ATLANTIC OCEAN

Three

South of the Grand Strand

Georgetown

FOR INFORMATION: The Georgetown Chamber of Commerce can answer most questions about the area. Call (843) 546-8436 or (800) 777-7705 or visit its website, www.tidelands.com.

The 270-year-old town of Georgetown has found a restored charm that is attracting more and more visitors. Located between Charleston and Myrtle Beach (it's sixty miles to Charleston, thirty-five to Myrtle Beach), it does not have a beach—but it does have some delightful attractions that make it well worth the attention of vacationers in the vicinity.

Some of the earliest sixteenth-century European settlements in South Carolina were made in this part of the coast near the point where the Sampit River flows into Winyah Bay. The city of Georgetown was laid out in 1729, and the original street plan remains unaltered. A thirty-two-block area with sixty buildings is listed on the National Register of Historic Places.

In the 1840s, Georgetown was at the heart of the nation's biggest rice-growing area. After the Civil War put an end to rice culture, it was lumber that fueled the local economy, and in 1914 Georgetown boasted the largest lumber-producing plant on the East Coast. International Paper built what became the largest kraft paper mill in the world here in the early 1940s. And the construction of Georgetown Steel further added to the town's surging economy. Though some local residents don't care to discuss it, Georgetown also had a reputation of another sort from the 1930s into the 1960s. It was the home to Sunset Lodge, the best-known brothel along the East Coast, which hosted numerous politicians, athletes, and visitors from all over the country who were passing through on the coastal highway. (It was closed by authorities in the '60s.)

That was then, however. Now, Georgetown draws visitors for its friendly businesses, a growing selection of nice shops and restaurants, and a rich, preserved history going back more than two centuries. It has been rated among the top 100 small towns in America.

Most visitors wind up on Front Street, which parallels the Sampit River and splits the main business district. There are some delightful and unusual shops here as well as many new, inexpensive restaurants which offer alfresco dining overlooking the surprisingly busy waters of the Sampit.

There are tours of historic homes and churches available by inquiring at the tourist welcome center, 1003 Front Street. The Rice Museum four blocks away on Front Street, which dates from 1841, has some good informational exhibits explaining the rice culture of the lowcountry, and visitors also can get information about the most interesting places to see around the city. Boat tours of the port and historic river plantations leave daily from docks along Front Street, providing delightful opportunities to view two-hundred-year-old lowcountry plantations otherwise impossible to see. The tours also give visitors a close-up look at wildlife, including alligators and eagles. The Georgetown Chamber of Commerce has lots of details on how and when to enjoy the many tours and facilities in this charming area.

There are some beautiful bed-and-breakfast inns in Georgetown, and the city has a variety of inexpensive chain motels for visitors. Anyone staying here will have to do some driving to get to a beach, however. The closest public beach would be at Pawleys Island, about ten miles to the north.

McClellanville

Heading south on US 17 from Georgetown brings travelers past the Grand Strand, but as the highway slips toward Charleston, it moves through towns with unique charms and unusual facilities well worth stopping to check out.

South of Georgetown, for instance, is the small village of McClellanville, which makes for another inviting stop. The town is about a mile off the highway down a lovely, twisting two-lane road. It's a shrimping community established shortly before the Civil War that has made a strong comeback from the devastation of Hurricane Hugo in 1989. That terrible storm destroyed the shrimp fleet, flattened many homes in the area, and produced rising floodwaters that very nearly engulfed hundreds of people who had crowded into a high school for safety. Some of the town's homes and churches are open for occasional tours, but for most people who come here the charm and solitude of the community will be sufficient reward for a brief visit. At the shrimp docks at the end of the road, you can get a close-up view of shrimp trawlers, clam dredges, and oyster boats and buy some terrific fresh seafood to take home. Beware, though: there can be a lot of activity at certain times because this is a business area and seafood is being unloaded and packed for delivery. Not all of the area is open to the public, so use common sense when visiting.

By the way, between Georgetown and McClellanville—the sign pointing to it is about thirteen miles south of Georgetown—is Hampton Plantation, the best-known and most accessible of the Santee River rice plantations of the eighteenth and nineteenth centuries. Now a state park, Hampton Plantation had its beginnings around 1700, and in 1791, George Washington stopped here (it's not just an apocryphal tale; his visit has been documented). Its most famous occupant was Archibald Rutledge, born in 1883, outdoorsman and author, who was the state's first poet laureate.)

There's a continuing rumor around these parts that Clark Gable, who played Captain Rhett Butler in the 1939 film of Margaret Mitchell's novel *Gone with the Wind,* paid a visit to Hampton shortly before the moviemaking began to check out some details of plantation life. The visit was never "officially" recorded, nor was that of other members of the technical crew who were said to have spent some time here also, and neither seems likely. While it's fun to contemplate Gable as tourist, Hampton's real history is rich enough to satisfy the most curious.

FOR INFORMATION on Hampton Plantation, call (843) 546-9361. The plantation and grounds are open for visitors daily.

● ●

Awendaw, Cape Romain, and Bull Island

A little over ten miles further south on US 17, the small community of Awendaw in Charleston County spreads thinly on both sides of the highway. Be sure to take a few minutes to go into the Sewee Visitor & Environment Education Center at Awendaw. Operated by the U.S. Forest Service and the U.S. Fish and Wildlife Service, it is the center for two important natural environmental areas along the coast: the Francis Marion National Forest and the 64,000-acre Cape Romain National Wildlife Refuge, established in 1932 as a haven for migratory birds.

The Sewee Visitor and Environmental Education Center is the gateway to wildlife refuges on Cape Romain and Bull Island. (Photograph by William W. Starr)

The center's staff can explain these amazing ecosystems in detail with special exhibits and an informative introductory film. There's also a special area where visitors can get a look at some of the rarely seen red wolves now being held for breeding. The species, once nearly decimated and endangered, is now being reintroduced into the wilds in a special federal program which began two decades ago in this vicinity.

FOR MORE INFORMATION on the wildlife refuge, call the Sewee Visitor & Environment Education Center at (843) 928-3368.

The center also is the place to get information about trips into the wildlife refuge, which occupies much of the coastal landscape between Georgetown and Charleston. Because access to the refuge is strictly limited, the only way to see it is by a thirty-minute passenger ferry ride. The ferries depart from Moore's Landing, a few miles south of the Sewee Center, for tours on Tuesdays, Thursdays, Fridays, and Saturdays from March 1 through November 30 and once a week (Saturdays) December 1 to February 29. These tours go to Bull Island, part of the Cape Romain environment and home to some 250 species of birds. Passengers have several hours to stroll along footpaths in the protected maritime forest and see such sights as the American bald eagle and loggerhead turtles. There's a charge for the tours.

Charter ferries are available to take visitors to other parts of the refuge, too. And several times during the year the Sewee Center sponsors boat tours to two isolated nineteenth-century lighthouses—now abandoned—on nearby Lighthouse Island. For details on times and fees, inquire at the center, which is open every day of the week except Mondays.

If you don't have time to stop at the center but you do want to grab the ferry at Moore's Landing, it's easy to do. The road leading to the landing is several miles south of Sewee on the left as you head south on US 17. The turnoff is marked. From the highway, it's 4.5 miles to the road, which dead-ends at the landing. If you're coming from Charleston, fifteen miles to the south, prepare for a right turn at the signs pointing to Moore's Landing.

BE SURE to check the ferry schedule; for information and reservations, call (843) 881-4582.

One word of caution: Except in the winter months, Bull Island is also a refuge for mosquitoes, tiny no-see-ums, and other devilish little critters who will drive you crazy scratching. It is an absolute necessity to bring insect repellent, and don't be shy about spreading it on. Don't forget the water, either, for the summer trips can leave you parched.

And finally, here's a tip for anyone traveling near Awendaw who's hungry. Not many people know about it, but the Sewee Restaurant on US 17 is well worth a stop. Originally a general store, its unprepossessing looks hide a slice of old lowcountry life inside. The food is wonderful, everything from she-crab soup to homemade pound cake. And the atmosphere is like hardly anything you've ever seen. Look for lots of locals here.

Four

The Charleston Area

Isle of Palms

FOR INFORMATION about the Isle of Palms, contact the Visitor Information Center, (843) 849-6154 or call City Hall, (843) 886-6328. A free vacation guide to the Isle of Palms, Wild Dunes, and Sullivan's Island may be requested by calling (800) 344-5105 or (800) 346-0606. For information about the Wild Dunes Resort, call (800) 845-8880, ext. 1 or (843) 886-2260. The website is www.WildDunes.com.

The first glimpse of the Isle of Palms when you're driving over the Highway 517 bridge is the prettiest view of the South Carolina coast you'll get outside of a low-flying airplane. As you hit the top of the bridge, the view spreads out like flower petals unfolding; the mighty Atlantic, stretching as far as the eye can sea, dozens of low-built homes lining the coast in both directions, the Intracoastal Waterway, visible on either side of the overpass, bisected by boats and jutting docks. It's a glorious sight. But don't stop on the bridge to enjoy the view; you're likely to get rammed by the fellow riding your bumper.

There's a lot of traffic out to the Isle of Palms. It's a very popular, active beach with a lot going on. That means in the summer months you can expect lots of cars and people, everyone eager to get there, get around once they're there, and then try to get back out. The confluence of those needs means the Isle of Palms is not a place for the faint-of-heart driver.

One of two islands lying to the north of Charleston, the Isle of Palms has a split personality. Part of it is cutoffs and beer, the other is slacks and martinis. They coexist, though occasionally with a little friction. Regardless, it's a beach with something for just about everyone's tastes.

The barrier island was the scene of attempts by the British to capture Charleston during the Revolutionary War. British General Sir Henry Clinton and his troops landed on the Isle of Palms (known then as Long Island) with the intention of using it as a staging point to attack Fort Moultrie on Sullivan's Island, a fort well-defended against bombardment from the sea but open to assault by land approaches from the north.

Clinton and his strategists believed the water between Long Island and Sullivan's Island—today known as Breach Inlet—was shallow enough to allow the soldiers to ford. They were wrong. It was then, as now, full of treacherous currents and much deeper than anticipated. The British army had to abandon its effort. "It was a bitter experience for Clinton," writes one historian with what is probably great understatement.

Charlestonians began building summer residences on Sullivan's Island in the nineteenth century. Development on the Isle of Palms came along a little later, however, and took a different path. Visitors began coming to the island starting in 1898 when it was accessible by water and a single railroad bridge. In the first decades of the twentieth century, summer homes began to appear, with growing numbers of people eager to use them, even though getting there could be an arduous journey. The island soon became something of a hub for social activity. There was a popular pavilion, and the Ferris wheel at the amusement park (which was operating as early as 1911) was said to be the highest in the world. Visitors could even enjoy the heart-pounding excitement of a flight in a biplane over the beach. A beachfront hotel, open in the summer months only, featured a dance hall and drew enthusiastic crowds to shimmy to the dance craze called the "Charleston." The hotel burned to the ground in the 1920s, though the dance became synonymous worldwide with the Jazz Age.

The opening of the John P. Grace Memorial Bridge over the Cooper River in 1929 was designed to improve access to Mount Pleasant, reached only by ferry before then, but it also increased traffic going to the beaches. During the heady days following the close of World War II, visitors and residences began appearing on the Isle of Palms in much greater numbers, however. In the 1960s and beyond, the island developed a reputation for an easygoing, anything-goes style of beach pleasures. Young people favored the Isle of Palms over its more sedate neighbor to the south, Sullivan's Island, as it offered a cheaper and livelier alternative. That's still pretty much the contrast between the two beaches: one staid, the other rockin'.

But—and it's a big but—there's a sea change when you drive to the north end of the Isle of Palms these days. That's where you'll run into one of the premier resort communities on the Atlantic coast: Wild Dunes, a 1,600-acre private retreat that bills itself as "Charleston's island resort." Anyone driving from the beery, noisy Windjammer on front beach at the Isle of Palms to the quiet, gated Wild Dunes might feel as if transported to another planet in the space of several miles. The resort occupies the northern end of the island and offers what you won't find elsewhere on the island: golf courses, along with some lavish homes and condos and pricey restaurants. There's plenty of fun inside Wild Dunes and it's wildly popular, but it's not necessarily the same kind of fun you'll discover outside the gates—and you'll pay more for it.

How to Get There

One of the reasons for the popularity of the Isle of Palms is its proximity to Charleston. It's about nine miles north of the city and easily approached in at least two ways. Coming from downtown Charleston, go over the Cooper River Bridge—another great view, but don't stop to savor it—and follow the signs to Coleman Boulevard (exit to the right coming off the bridge), which takes you into Mount Pleasant. Several miles down the boulevard, signs will direct you to the right toward Sullivan's Island and the Isle of Palms. You'll arrive on Sullivan's Island first. As you pull into the town, turn to the left on Highway 703 (there are signs pointing to the Isle of Palms) and drive straight. You'll cross over Breach Inlet and be on the Isle of Palms in just 2 miles.

As a possibly faster alternative that bypasses Sullivan's, try this: coming off the Cooper River Bridge, go straight on US 17 North. You'll pass the Mark Clark Expressway (US 526) on your way to Highway 517 on the right, which leads directly to the Isle of Palms. The trip from downtown Charleston can take about thirty minutes depending on traffic. Avoid morning and afternoon rush hours if possible; traffic can back up around the bridges and expressways.

Coming from Interstate 26 in North Charleston, take the US 526 Mark Clark Expressway exit to Mount Pleasant. Then follow the signs to the Isle of Palms, which takes you to US 17 North and then 517. That's the way to come if you've arrived by plane. The airport is a little less than a half hour away from the Isle of Palms.

Where to Stay

The Isle of Palms has most elements of accommodations to be found at beaches except for large high-rise hotels. Look for places like the Holiday Inn Express and Sea Cabins. There are condo/apartments and homes on the beachfront and toward the back of the island that rent for moderate sums compared to the likes of similar accommodations at nearby Wild Dunes or Kiawah. In fact, among South Carolina beaches, rentals at the Isle of Palms are

Wild Dunes, a resort on the Isle of Palms north of Charleston, offers two and a half miles of beach, luxurious villas, restaurants, a conference center, and two spectacular golf courses. (Courtesy South Carolina Department of Parks, Recreation & Tourism)

among the more reasonably priced. Access to all is easy; this beach is not a gated locale. There are real estate agents and rental agents centered around the business district.

At Wild Dunes, the prices go up, but so does the style of accommodations. There are very expensive condominiums or homes to rent on the 2^1/2-mile beachfront or bordering the golf courses or on the marshes. As a rule, the farther away from the beach you go, the lower the prices—relatively speaking. In addition, there's Wild Dunes' new Boardwalk Inn, with adjacent villas and attractive pools all done up in the manner of the traditional beach boardwalk. The beachfront hotel has received high accolades from guests and national accommodations rating services like Mobil and AAA. It has upscale rooms, including even a presidential suite on the top floor with views and accoutrements suited to a president—one with deep pockets, that is. Wild

Dunes is a gated community, and access is limited to residents and guests. There's a guard station at the entrance with passes or stickers necessary for admission.

And for guests who really value their privacy, there's Ocean Point at the northern tip of Wild Dunes. This is a private gated community within the Wild Dunes gated community. There's no guard house, just a tall gate requiring coded entry. Since it's difficult to get inside, there's no way of telling whether there's yet another private, gated community within Ocean Point. In any event, it's the place to be if you want to keep the ordinary Wild Dunes riffraff out of your yard.

Where to Eat

Conventional wisdom decrees that if you head for the beach, your stomach had better brace for cheeseburgers and beer. And while you can find plenty of places to munch a burger and quaff a brew or two, and hear some beach music while you're doing it, the fact is that the Isle of Palms has some pretty good dining establishments, which attract even Charleston residents for an occasional outing.

The Boathouse, located at Breach Inlet on the road to Sullivan's Island, attracts a full house just about every weekend. The menu includes plenty of fresh seafood (the restaurant is located on Hamlin Creek) and a lively atmosphere. In a small strip mall called Island Center, you'll find the Long Island Café, popular with visitors and residents and specializing in American cuisine. On the north end of the island, at Wild Dunes Marina, is another popular seafood restaurant.

Without question the best-known establishment at the Isle of Palms, however, didn't get its reputation for its food. The Windjammer, in the middle of the island on the beachfront—anyone can give you directions, or just follow the young crowd—is the place to go to have fun with other mostly young people. The two-story building can't be missed; it's got a large, sandy volleyball court right next door to it where denizens of the beery interior can slip out for a little sun and sweat. Young men and women ooze out of the Windjammer in summer. It's got the best rock bands playing nightly, and the combination of noise, beer, and wall-to-wall gyrating and semi-naked people can make for delightfully combustible scenes. Coats and ties are not required. This is, needless to say, not exactly the place to bring families with small children. There are other restaurants/bars close by along the beachfront offering some of the same pleasures, such as Banana Cabana, but the Windjammer is the one with the longest pedigree. A lot of partygoers head there because—or in spite of the fact—that's where their parents went.

There are other places, including a fast-food chain restaurant, where you can grab something cheap and quick. Otherwise, it's back to Charleston.

At Wild Dunes, there are several dining options. At the resort's Boardwalk Inn, guests can enjoy upscale menus blending French and American cuisines at The Grill. In addition, more casual dining is available at Edgar's, which overlooks a golf course, and at Dunes Deli and Pizzeria. For evening meals, reservations are suggested at Edgar's and the Boardwalk.

If you're not staying at Wild Dunes but want to eat at one of the restaurants there, drive to the gate and tell the guard. You should be admitted without any delay, particularly if you have called ahead for a reservation.

What to Do

Well, there's sunbathing. There's swimming. There's bike riding. There's windsurfing. There's deep-sea fishing. There's sea-gazing. There's sitting on the porch reading a good book. And there's heading down to the Windjammer to listen to some music and get a cool one. What else did you come to the beach for?

The Isle of Palms County Park—just beyond the traffic light when you arrive from Highway 517—has a pay parking area for day-trippers, changing rooms, restrooms, and easy beach access. It's not very big and fills up quickly in the summer months. If you're arriving for a day visit only, expect to look long and hard for parking spaces. There are several designated pay lots around the retail area, along with metered spaces on the street. The police enforce the parking laws to the letter, so if you meter expires or you're parked where the signs say not to park, you will pay the price (which can, in some instances, mean towing). There are places to park along the streets extending away from the center of the island; just follow the posted directions.

If you'd like to go to some Sunday services, you'll find on the island St. Marks Evangelical Lutheran Church, First United Methodist Church, and the Isle of Palms Baptist Church.

On the south end of the Isle of Palms is Breach Inlet. There are limited parking spaces here, but this is not the place to stop for anything but beach strolling. Signs warn against swimming or wading because of the dangerous currents. The threat of drowning is a very serious one, and while there is a $200 fine for violations, there is the possibility of a worse fate for those who disregard the warning. If you want to get in the water, do it elsewhere.

On the north end of the Isle of Palms at Wild Dunes is a resort full of activities including meeting and convention facilities. There are two eighteen-hole golf courses acclaimed among the finest in America, both designed by Tom Fazio. Wild Dunes Links is a 6,722-yard, par 72 course. The finishing holes are on the Atlantic Ocean with ocean breezes, large dunes, and natural hazards

Children admire an elaborate fourteen-point kite on the beach at the Isle of Palms. (Photograph © 2001 Robert Clark)

making play particularly challenging. The Harbor Course is a 6,446, par 72 layout, directly on the Intracoastal Waterway. In fact, golfers have holes to play from one island to another across the waters of Morgan Creek. Wild Dunes also offers PROLINK, a personal electronic service. It's a little device located in the golf cart that computes exact yardage, layout overviews, distances to each hole, and tips on how best to play the hole. It's the next best thing to an experienced caddy (although not nearly as chatty). There are fully stocked pro shops, and golf instruction is available for beginners or near-pros in need of touchups.

The Wild Dunes Tennis Center is ranked among the country's finest, with nineteen courts including a stadium court with seating for 350 spectators (in case your game merits that sort of attention). *Tennis* magazine rates the center among its "Top 50 U.S. Tennis Resorts," and the center has hosted the U.S.

Men's Clay court championships and the Southern Seniors Tournament. Pro shops and lessons help to round out the complete net experience.

Wild Dunes also has a full-service marina located just outside the resort on the Intracoastal Waterway.

Shopping

The Isle of Palms isn't exactly a shopper's paradise, but there are stores to take care of most of your typical beach needs. Want some shades? How about a beach towel? Maybe some groceries, or fill up the car with gas? No problem. Want to mail a letter? There's a post office here. Need an architect? Just a short walk from the beachfront. How about a travel agent? Or a liquor store? The Isle of Palms can accommodate you easily. And if you're running short and need a giant supermarket or a large pharmacy, they are located just five minutes away over the Highway 517 bridge leading back toward Charleston.

Wild Dunes has its own shops selling a little more high-end merchandise, for the most part, along with the golf and tennis pro shops. Unless you're a guest, however, these won't be accessible. (If you want to check them out, plan to go to one of the restaurants—which will get you in—then hang around the shops after you finish your meal.)

For department stores and greater shopping variety, head back toward Mount Pleasant and Charleston.

What to Wear

The Isle of Palms is a casual beach, and beachwear is acceptable just about everywhere, though in the more upscale restaurants you'll need a shirt and shoes (or sandals). If you're going to the Windjammer, a swimsuit will do nicely. At Wild Dunes, of course, there are dress requirements, and while jackets and ties are not necessary, beachwear is not acceptable in some circumstances (like dining at The Grill in the evening, for instance). Phone ahead if you're in doubt.

When to Go

Just about everyone goes in the summer months. That's when the temperatures are highest and the crowds are the biggest. Weekends especially get pretty hectic with sunlovers, from toddlers to granddads, all over the streets and beaches. Expect temperatures in the 90s regularly, broken occasionally by late afternoon thunderstorms. If you're playing golf or tennis at Wild Dunes, keep plenty of water handy.

For many people, the spring and fall are the best times at the beach. In the fall, particularly, the air temperatures are milder, sea temperatures are still warm, and the crowds are fewer, whether you're on the beach or the golf course. And even in the winter months, the temperatures seldom go below the 30s at night, and the days—which can be sunny with temperatures in the 50s or even 60s—are pleasant for beach-walking or hitting tennis balls. The rates for rental units also go down considerably during the winter, making the beach particularly attractive for the budget-minded.

Sullivan's Island

FOR INFORMATION call the Sullivan's Island Town Hall at (843) 883-3198. For a free vacation guide to Sullivan's Island, the Isle of Palms, and Wild Dunes, call (800) 344-5105 or (800) 346-0606. For general information about the Charleston area, including Sullivan's Island, call (843) 853-8000 or go to www.charlestoncvb.com.

Sullivan's Island, a narrow sandbar just north of the city of Charleston, is South Carolina's "history" island, the oldest beach resort in the area. It has been at the center of not one but three upheavals in the American past—the American Revolution, the importation of slaves, and the Civil War—and it has been historically the most fashionable of the beaches surrounding Charleston.

If fashionable has sometimes seemed to mean snobby to some, then a lot of Charlestonians might well say, "So be it." The fact is, though, that Folly Beach to the south and the Isle of Palms to the north have earned reputations as rowdier, coarser, livelier summer beaches. If you want to boogie on the beach, those two are eager to embrace you. If, however, there's a quieter, more reserved, streak in you, and you want to see where wealthy Charlestonians used to go to get away from the travails of city life, Sullivan's is ready to appease your preference. But it's not just a case of money. After all, you can spend more at nearby Wild Dunes or Kiawah. Buying a home on Sullivan's used to be about as difficult as getting a ticket to a New York Knicks game. With changes wrought by Hurricane Hugo in 1989, it's not quite that way any longer (though prices have skyrocketed). But Sullivan's manages to maintain something of that hard-to-define but oh-so-important Charleston "attitude." Call it tradition, or maybe a unique kind of lifestyle. Whatever you say about it, Sullivan's is as different from Folly Beach and the Isle of Palms as the Kennedys are from the rest of Massachusetts.

The naming of Sullivan's Island goes back to the founding of the Carolina colony in 1670. The captain of the *Carolina*, the first English ship to bring settlers to what would be Charles Town, was Capt. Florence O'Sullivan, who became a member of the provincial parliament two years later. He was authorized to place a cannon at the southern end of the island, and a good thing: it was used when the French and Spanish attempted an invasion in 1706.

The island figured prominently in history in the early days of the American rebellion against Great Britain. As Charleston grew and prospered in the eighteenth century with wealthy planters and merchants, so too did the city's importance to the American colonies. At the time of the Revolution, Charleston was second only to Boston as the major Atlantic port. That made it a target for the British when the colonies declared their independence in 1776.

At that time, there were a few structures known to exist on Sullivan's, which was accessible from Charleston only by boat. And some of those buildings were said to have washed up in the Cooper River when the great hurricane of 1752 hit the lowcountry.

To aid in the defense against an anticipated British attack on the exposed Charleston Harbor, South Carolinians rushed to construct a fort made of palmetto tree logs taken from nearby Dewees Island. Gen. William Moultrie took command of the more than four hundred men assigned to duty in the fort. Meanwhile, the northern end of the island (facing what is now the Isle of Palms) had another force of seven hundred men prepared to face an assault from that direction. The British planned to attack the fort from the sea and move in soldiers from the north to assail the fort's defenders from the land.

Their land invasion flopped because the waters of Breach Inlet were too deep and strong. The attack on the fort also failed. Shots from the British fleet fell harmlessly into the spongy palmetto logs. The British eventually withdrew, suffering the loss of one ship and more than a hundred men. American losses totaled less than half that.

The action was important for the state, and not merely for repelling the invaders. The fort was named Fort Moultrie in honor of its commander (and can be visited today), while the success of the palmetto logs in holding the British at bay led to their being affixed to the state flag, whereupon South Carolina became known as the Palmetto State. Unfortunately, that wasn't the end of the story. The British returned in 1780 and laid siege to the city, capturing and holding it until withdrawing shortly before the surrender to American forces under George Washington at Yorktown in 1782.

Before the Revolution, and extending into the nineteenth century, Sullivan's Island became what historians have called the Ellis Island of Black Americans. According to eighteenth-century law, ships carrying slaves were required to first land on Sullivan's Island to deposit their human cargo. Once there, the enslaved—men, women and children—were taken to what was called a "pest house," where they were kept for weeks until they had been examined and approved by a health inspector. "If the new Americans were still alive at the end of the quarantine, they would be released to their captors and sold at auction in Charleston, five miles away," wrote historian Edward Ball, author of *Slaves in the Family.*

There are estimates that between 1700 and 1755 more than 40 percent of the Africans who were brought to the colonies came through Charleston. Those who died at sea during their perilous journey were thrown overboard; those who died in quarantine probably were buried in mass graves.

Edgar Allan Poe was a brooding, intense eighteen-year-old assigned to a military unit at Fort Moultrie in 1827–28. He spent a little more than a year on Sullivan's Island, and, according to some sources, was fond of walking in storms. Later, using images he observed during his stay, he wrote a blood-chilling story about pirate treasure, "The Gold Bug," published in 1843. There, he described the island: "This island is a very singular one. It consists of little else than the sea sand, and it is about three miles long . . . . It is separated from the mainland by a scarcely perceptible creek, oozing its way through a wilderness of reeds and slime, a favorite resort of the marsh hen." Poe's visit is memorialized today in streets called Poe Avenue, Raven Street, and Gold Bug Avenue.

After South Carolina seceded from the Union, the Civil War began in Charleston in April 1861 with the firing on Union-held Fort Sumter (another popular stop for visitors to the Charleston area these days) in the middle of Charleston Harbor. The first shots were fired at 3:30 A.M. on April 12, 1861. Within an hour, cannons at Fort Moultrie and other forts in the harbor began their bombardment. On April 14, the beleaguered defenders of Fort Sumter surrendered. Over the next four years, Sullivan's Island was occupied by various Confederate military and militia units, and the fort saw occasional action defending the harbor against attacks. In February 1865, Union soldiers occupied Charleston, and the war ended for the city and the islands around it.

In the latter part of the nineteenth century, Charlestonians began building summer homes on the beach as a refuge against the oppressive semitropical heat in the city. With no bridge, residents headed to Sullivan's from Charleston in a variety of boats and ferries over the Cooper River. As the turn of the century approached, well-off Charlestonians, their families and guests would pack up belongings and take the servants along as they escaped the city for three months of beach time at Sullivan's. Old photographs show that some visitors even took along the family cow. Some beachgoers arrived by boat. Most came on carriages and then trolleys and automobiles through Mount Pleasant when bridges were built over the marshes and creeks leading to Sullivan's Island.

In the early years of the twentieth century, Sullivan's was a far cry from what visitors see today. Most witnesses call it "a quaint seaside village." Edward Ball wrote of his family's life on the island: "Year-round residents like ourselves lived in creaky cottages on the ocean, or along the handful of streets off the water. The loudest sound during the day came from the crashing waves, and at night from the frogs that sang in the gullies." The beach was wide, and cars were permitted to drive across it.

The opening of the Grace Memorial Bridge in 1929 spanning the Cooper River eased access to Mount Pleasant, the Isle of Palms, and Sullivan's Island and led to the anticipated rise of people using those areas. While the Isle of Palms attracted day-trippers, Sullivan's remained primarily the haunt of the "old" Charlestonians, whose occupancy of the island was interrupted only temporarily by World War II.

That continued with only modest change until 1989 when Hurricane Hugo ripped the island, causing extensive damage and requiring an enormous rebuilding program. That storm in its way "democratized" Sullivan's Island a bit. Some old-time residents decided to leave; new, younger people arrived. Among today's residents are Josephine Humphreys (*Dreams of Sleep; Rich in Love*) and Dorthea Frank (*Sullivan's Island*). While Sullivan's remains a bastion of fine old homes, many have been rebuilt. And there are many new ones, too. Once, "For Sale" signs were a no-no. Now they can be seen all over (if you have to ask the price, you can't afford them). Grand old wooden cottages now face brick and concrete mansions. What was a quaint seaside village has become a gentrified beachfront community, yet one that still exudes its own special kind of charm.

How to Get There

From Charleston, cross over the Cooper River Bridge to Mount Pleasant, exiting the bridge on the right, following the signs pointing to Coleman Boulevard and Mount Pleasant (Highway 703). A couple of miles later, signs will direct you to the right toward Sullivan's on 703. Within five minutes (unless you run into a bridge open to allow boats to pass along the Intracoastal Waterway) you'll be at the middle of the island. Depending on the volume of traffic out of Charleston, that journey can take about thirty minutes.

Coming from the airport, it's best to get on the Mark Clark Expressway (Interstate 526) headed toward Mount Pleasant. Take the exit to Georgetown and the Isle of Palms (US 17 North). Stay on 17 North for two miles, then turn to the right on Highway 517, which takes you to the Isle of Palms. At the traffic light on the island, turn right onto Highway 703, which crosses Breach

Inlet and deposits you on Sullivan's Island. The trip from the Charleston airport to Sullivan's usually will take about a half hour.

Where to Stay

Sullivan's Island has the sense of an "old" beach about it, and while accommodations are limited compared to the Isle of Palms and Folly Beach, many of them ooze old-fashioned charm. For the most part, Sullivan's remains a residential beach, and most rentals are homes that absentee owners are renting by the week or month, or for an entire summer in some instances. Many old-timers recall the Sandpiper Inn, a fixture for summer guests for many years. It's still there in a weather-beaten, block-long structure, but it is now long-term apartments only. There are no hotels or motels on Sullivan's, and don't waste time looking for bed-and-breakfasts, either. There are scattered rental units, cottages and increasing numbers of homes to rent, but everything has been kept generally to the scale of the island, even as the island changes as part of its post-Hugo metamorphosis. It's not for nothing, however, that the Isle of Palms and Folly Beach are classified "cities" and Sullivan's Island is a town.

Where to Eat

Sullivan's Island may not be a gourmand's heaven, but there are some interesting, eclectic restaurants and pubs on the island. Not all of them may be open during the winter months, so be sure to check if you're visiting in January or February. There are no chain, fast-food establishments, which is unquestionably part of the charm of this traffic-light island.

Around Station 22 (which designates stop No. 22 on the old trolley route) are several places to dine and drink. Station 22, Dunleavy's Pub, Bert's Bar, and the Dog House Grille are popular; nearby are Gibson Café and Saltwater Grill. All are quite reasonably priced, boast intriguing atmospheres and promise (and deliver) lots of fun and that certain Sullivan's style for the locals and visitors. Just across Breach Inlet—it's actually on the Isle of Palms—is the Boathouse, a restaurant on the water that serves well-prepared fresh seafood and has become one of the most popular restaurants along the coast. For more variety than that, you'll have to head back to Mount Pleasant and Charleston or bring your own groceries.

What to Do

There are no amusement parks on Sullivan's and not much at all in the way of night life. So if you're headed in this direction, you'd better be prepared to enjoy the simpler pleasures of the beach. Like getting a suntan. Or body surfing. Or reading. Or dozing. It's a great place for families, though teenagers may want a little more action. The beach is very nice, however, and most visitors find Sullivan's a wonderful place to shed some of the stress and anxiety of the non-beach world.

If you're renting a house at the beach, you'll have beach access. If you are visiting during the day, you'll find a limited number of designated parking areas with marked paths pointing you to the beach, but be sure to follow the parking rules carefully; they are strictly enforced. Beach access paths are clearly marked up and down the island with adjacent areas where parallel parking only is permitted. Don't even think about parking on someone's yard. The police will be there before you get your beach towel unfolded.

Visitors with youngsters in tow might want to stop by the Sullivan's Island Foundation Park, two blocks south of the main intersection, what passes for the center of the town. It's got a playground area for children, a gazebo for occasional concerts, basketball courts, and a short walking path. Nearby is a branch of the Charleston County Public Library, well worth a visit even if you don't intend to check out a book. It's housed in one of the many old coastal fortifications found throughout the island. It looks like a bunker—in fact, it is a bunker—and it's a most unlikely locale for a library. The chances are everyone will get a chuckle from the appearance. It's off Ion Avenue at Station 20 (the streets which are perpendicular to the ocean are called stations, the numbers getting higher as you drive toward the Isle of Palms).

Ion Avenue (it's pronounced IE-un), by the way, has a bit of an interesting history. According to Claude and Irene Neuffer, it was named for Colonel Jacob I'on, a veteran of the Mexican War who enjoyed quite a reputation for his hospitality in the area. Officers from nearby Fort Moultrie spent much time at his home, presumably quaffing a few alcoholic beverages. One of the most frequent visitors was a young red-haired lieutenant named William T. Sherman, who would make a memorable return visit in 1865 when he applied his "total war" philosophy to many parts of South Carolina during the final months of the Civil War.

Sullivan's Island has always played an important role in coastal defense. Fort Moultrie at the southern end of the island was the first fortification, but in the nineteenth and twentieth centuries, additional fortifications were constructed up and down the island. The remnants—and in a few cases the structures themselves—are easily viewed today, and they are one of the most fascinating sights on Sullivan's.

Through the cobweb of streets (or stations), the steel fortifications protrude, some dating back to the Spanish-American War, most to World War I or World War II. At one of them, Battery Thomson from the Second World War, fire and rescue units now conduct their training exercises. There is a

*Tourists climb to an observation deck built atop an old World War I
bunker at Fort Moultrie. (Photograph © 2001 Robert Clark)*

bunker next to the lighthouse at the United States Coast Guard station; it's not
open to the public, however. To the north end, a number of batteries and
bunkers have been converted into private, underground homes, their front
entrances protruding from massive hills. They have been resurrected and
given a suburban glaze, and the contrasts are visually arresting. For some of
the most unusual ones, look around Station 28 and Station 31.

Fort Moultrie, of course, is the most popular attraction on the island and
a wonderful place to stop and savor some of the rich history of the coast. The
National Park Service maintains the fort. The existing structure was completed in 1809, the third fort to occupy the site, and it has been carefully
restored to show not only South Carolina's military role but to portray the full
effort at coastal defense over the years. There are park rangers on hand to
answer questions, and an easy walk through the fort and grounds affords not
only information but exercise as well. There is a small fee; the fort is open daily

during daylight hours. To get to Fort Moultrie, turn right on Middle Street when you get to the center of town; the fort is just five minutes away.

Several churches are close by while you're at Sullivan's, including Sullivan's Island Baptist Church, Stella Maris Roman Catholic Church, Holy Cross Episcopal Church, and Sunrise Presbyterian Church. There's also a post office and a gas station. For a supermarket, however, head back toward Mount Pleasant. But should you have need of a psychologist, ophthalmologist, or physical therapist, fear not: they all have offices on the island.

There are no golf courses on Sullivan's Island. There is a private boat landing to the south end, but there are homes to rent that have docks where boats can be tied up and which also serve as effective platforms for snaring some delicious crabs.

Shopping

A few shops along the Middle Street "downtown" sell the usual beach goods—towels, sandals, beach balls, sunglasses, etc.—but that's about it. Hardly anyone seems to be interested in seeing a large retail area developed on Sullivan's Island, so for the foreseeable future, shopping here will be very limited. It's just not why people come to this island.

What to Wear

You're pretty much on your own on Sullivan's Island. It's your home, and you can wear what you please. During the summer, less is better, of course, and only if you're heading to a restaurant or some other indoor activity do you need to be concerned with anything other than beach attire. Use common sense, however, and don't offend your neighbors.

When to Go

When are you free? Sullivan's Island, like other beaches along the South Carolina coast, gets plenty hot in the summer, and that's one of the reasons why most people are here at that time of year. Finding rental units can be very difficult, though the beaches hardly ever seem crowded. Expect temperatures into the 90s frequently and cross your fingers for a little sea breeze. In the spring and fall, the temperatures are milder, though they tend toward the warm side, and it gets a little bit easier to find a place to stay. The brief winter months also have their share of very mild weather, and some visitors swear that's the best time to come. If that's your choice, be sure to bring along a coat or sweater, however; walking along the beach in February can be a delight, but it can be very chilly, too. There is a reason you'll find a sign at Breach Inlet declaring "Bridge Freezes Before Road." It has been known to happen, though not often.

Folly Beach

TO CONTACT the City of Folly Beach, call (843) 588-2447. For information about beach rentals, call (843) 588-2325. For a twenty-four-hour camera view of surfing conditions at Folly, go to the website follysurfcam.com. For general information about the Charleston area, including Folly, call (843) 853-8000 or go online at www.charlestoncvb.com.

We don't know what the Bohicket Indians might have called it when they were sole users of the beach in the early seventeenth century. But it's had several names since, none expressing what might seem the ideal vacation virtues of fun and ease. Dictionaries tell us a "folly" was an island with a discernible treeline, as opposed to a barren desert island. Not much romance there. Some early arrivals at the island called it Coffin Land. Then it was Folly Island. Today, it's just Folly Beach. If the name suggests foolishness, it also has a hint of fun about it, and Folly embraces both of those characteristics.

If a beach can be said to be a "survivor," Folly certainly qualifies. It has endured through hurricanes, storms, human-inflicted abuse and neglect not to mention motorcycle gangs and surfer dudes. The unofficial bumper sticker found on more than few cars along the beach reads, "Welcome to the Edge of America." There are more old Volkswagen buses to be found still running on Folly than any other beach in South Carolina.

Folly has a rich history filled with pirates and Civil War soldiers and even George Gershwin. It has a reputation as the liveliest, most rambunctious, and most public beach in the Charleston area—indulgent at times, perhaps, but accepting to all manner of lifestyles. It has no golf courses—something of a rarity for any beach part of South Carolina's tee-it-up coastal culture. There are no large resort hotels, no high-rise condos (well, maybe some brand new midrise units), no fancy restaurants.

It has a beach that sometimes isn't. The U.S. Army Corps of Engineers routinely dredges sand and pours it on the beach to build up what has been washed down. Winter storms—and sometimes mighty hurricanes—come along and tear it down. "We gain a lot of beach in the summer, and then we lose even more in the winter storms," says one longtime resident. It's been that way for most of the last century when the engineers first built jetties in Charleston Harbor to the north of Folly. Their plan helped deepen the main channel through Charleston Harbor, but it produced erosion that has toyed with Folly Beach ever since.

For instance, since the middle of the eighteenth century, there has been a lighthouse on Morris Island, the low-lying island just above (or east) of Folly that faces into Charleston Harbor. When the construction of the jetties in the harbor was completed in 1895, the existing lighthouse was 2,700 feet from the shoreline. By 1940, the ocean lapped at its base. Now that lighthouse stands in the Atlantic, more than 1,700 feet offshore, but there have been efforts to save it from disappearing into the ocean. Folly has felt the erosion in other ways, too. In some years at high tide, there has been no beach. The ocean has washed up, occasionally under and beyond, beachfront housing, destroying and re-creating at the same time.

But the beach renourishment program has paid off in several ways. It seems to have given Folly something of a new life. With assurances of a beach, high tide or not—and no matter how expensively maintained—many of the 1,400 year-round residents have experienced resurgent pride in their homes, and visitors have returned in growing numbers. It didn't hurt that insurance money floated to the island for major rebuilding projects after Hurricane Hugo roared through in 1989. Prices for property on what was once the cheapest beach on the coast have soared upward, though homes at Folly Beach still can be acquired for a fraction of the cost at Kiawah Island to the south and Sullivan's Island to the north. In its way, Folly is slowly experiencing a period of gentrification as the wealthier move in and the poorer move out.

Evidence of the resurgence of Folly is not hard to miss. New homes dot the landscape. A new wooden pier stretching over 1,000 feet into the Atlantic opened in 1995, a joy for fishermen and strollers alike. Beachcombers can sit in the shade (or the sun) at a restaurant at the pier and watch the activity below. Behind them is McKelvin's Surf Shop, rebuilt after Hurricane Hugo slammed Folly in 1989 but still a name known to surfers all over the country since the 1960s.

Folly has some of the best surfing on the East Coast, and many East Coast Surfing Association competitions have been held here. There was a time in the late 1960s and early 1970s when surfers and residents clashed over issues of noise and disruption. Eventually certain areas of the beach, in the "washout" zone to the north (or east) end of the island, were designated for surfers. Just about any time of the year, now, you'll find members of the surfing clan clutching their boards just offshore looking for the perfect wave. It's one of the sights that makes Folly unique among South Carolina beaches.

The look of Folly is, in a word, undisciplined. Expensive new single-family homes bump up against ramshackle huts. Aging apartments face off against sleek condos. Comfortable, suburbanlike ranch houses back up to three-story brick and tabby mansions. It's not quite as quirky as it used to be, perhaps, but Folly definitely has an "attitude."

Everywhere on the island there are numerous small public parking areas and beach access ramps. At the south (west) end of the island is Folly Beach County Park, boasting an amazing 4,000 feet of some of the nicest beach on the coast, available to anyone who pays a minimal parking fee. Its construction further demonstrates new vitality of Folly. At the height of summer, all of the access points fill up by midmorning as day-trippers from Charleston, a mere twenty-minute drive away, join tourists from other states in heading for the sun, surf, and sand. That kind of access makes Folly unusual on South Carolina's widely privatized coast.

Folly, one of South Carolina's barrier islands, extends for a little over $6\frac{1}{2}$ miles from east to west, from the county park at the west end to just above the prime surfing area to the east. At its widest, the island is about one-half mile between the oceanfront and the winding Folly River at the back. The housing density is considerably lower than might be expected. Away from the beachfront, homes spread out on shaded lots paralleling Ashley Avenue and Arctic Avenue, the main east-west front streets.

William Rivers was the first owner of Folly Island, acquiring title in a grant from Governor John Archdale in 1696, twenty-six years after the first English settlers dropped anchor a few miles away to found what would become Charleston in the colony of Carolina. The island changed ownership many times over the next three hundred years as the Native Americans slowly receded away from the coastal settlements. The earliest white inhabitants apparently were on the island before the 1730s. They may have come ashore unexpectedly and unintentionally, victims of one of the many shipwrecks recorded off the coast. That might also explain where the name Coffin Land came from. In 1832, a ship stricken with cholera among its crew and passengers ran ashore on Folly Beach. The survivors were quarantined to prevent the spread of the deadly contagious disease. Twenty-one people died once they got to the island, but the spread was contained.

A few years later, with the outbreak of the Civil War in 1861, it was difficult to contain the violence that occurred on and near Folly Island. The first shots of the war—colloquially referred to as "the late unpleasantness" by more genteel Southerners—were fired into Union-held Fort Sumter in Charleston Harbor from Confederate forts surrounding it. One of those forts was on Morris Island.

In the war's early years, Folly was the launching point for Union attempts to capture Charleston, something that did not occur until the final days of the war in 1865. When Confederates abandoned Folly and consolidated their command on Morris Island, somewhere between 6,000 and 10,000 Union

The Morris Island Lighthouse is visible—though no longer accessible on land—from the old Coast Guard Station on Folly Beach. (Photograph © 2001 Robert Clark)

soldiers occupied Folly as part of the federal government's seizure of the South Carolina sea islands. There, on what must have been an exotic location for men who had seldom ventured beyond their hometowns in the Northeast and Midwest, soldiers trained, lived, and worked. The experience left some of them with vivid if hardly flattering memories.

"If there is a worse place than these sand islands, I don't want to see it," one soldier wrote home. Units from Indiana, Pennsylvania, and the New England states complained of midsummer temperatures which—then as now—soared past 100 degrees. Some regarded the tiny sand fleas which would bite unrelentingly as a worse enemy than the Confederates. "It did look a piece of Folly to try to live on such an island," wrote one weary Pennsylvanian to a no doubt sympathetic family back home.

Folly was the jumping-off point for one of the Civil War's best-known incidents. On the evening of July 18, 1863, colored troops of the 54th Massachusetts made a dramatic charge against Confederate-held Fort Wagner on the northern tip of Morris Island. That heroic but abortive attack was memorialized in the acclaimed 1989 film *Glory.* Sergeant William H. Carney was one of the 54th who charged the fort when he found the national flag lying on the ground, its bearer wounded. Carney grabbed the flag and continued the attack up to the fort's sloping wall, where he too was wounded. Later, Sergeant

Carney would become the first African American soldier to be awarded the Congressional Medal of Honor. Fort Wagner, eventually abandoned by Confederates as they withdrew into Charleston, no longer exists.

It was not until after World War I that Folly Island fell into its first period of prosperity. There was no bridge to link Charleston to the beaches to the north of the city until 1929, but beginning in 1920, there was a private road reaching all the way to Folly. Soon after, the beach became the biggest coastal attraction in the lowcountry. It could be reached by private car on that narrow, rutted dirt road—the trip took is said to have taken two hours most of the time—or by steamer or bus. Thousands came. Some stayed to buy houses, which could be purchased for as little as $580. In 1927, some 70,000 people spent part of their summer at Folly. For the first time, the lucky ones had electricity for their lights. Still, Folly remained largely undeveloped.

DuBose Heyward—the white Charleston author best known for his 1925 novel *Porgy,* inspired by a real-life crippled black beggar who got around on a goat cart—purchased a summer home on Folly that he called "Follywood." His collaboration with the composer George Gershwin led to the creation of the opera *Porgy and Bess.* In June of 1934, Gershwin accepted Heyward's invitation to come to Folly to work on the musical score. Gershwin stayed at a small beachfront cottage, battling the heat and mosquitoes, working late into the night at an upright piano that, like the drinking water, had been brought over from Charleston.

The Gershwin cottage washed away in a hurricane in 1940. But Heyward's home, considerably improved over its 1930s condition, still can be viewed at Folly. Gershwin left the island in August of 1934, and just over a year later *Porgy and Bess* had its modestly successful world premiere performances in New York. Now it is regarded by many as America's greatest opera and has been performed at the Metropolitan in New York and at other major opera houses around the globe.

During the 1930s and '40s, Folly enjoyed a reputation as a haven for artists, and growing numbers of visitors found plenty of entertainment, too. During the Depression era, bootleggers and rum-runners profited from steady business at the nightclubs that sprang up along the causeway leading to Folly. At the beach, some of the nation's best-known musicians appeared, including the big bands led by the likes of Tommy Dorsey, Artie Shaw, and Harry James. Dance contests were the rage for residents and tourists alike.

The years after the end of World War II were good to Folly. The return of prosperity and the end of wartime restrictions led to a building spurt and more visitors. The boardwalk and amusement park gave the beach a kind of Coney

Island feel that discouraged the residential development. Problems with erosion continued along with some unexpected new concerns ranging from unruly behavior of some visitors to political corruption. In the 1960s and '70s, in the aftermath of damaging hurricanes, the failure of ambitious plans for expansion and modernization, and a series of tragic murders of young women, Folly fell on hard times. It was incorporated in 1973 as part of an effort to refocus the town's future. Property values dropped off the realtor's charts along with the number of visitors. By the 1980s, Folly had the reputation of having the cheapest beach property on the Atlantic coast, a label not intended as any sort of compliment.

Ironically, it took another vicious force of nature—the terrible Hurricane Hugo in September 1989—to launch a new period of revitalization. Hugo and its 135-mile-an-hour winds and surging tides took a vicious bite out of South Carolina, killing 26 people and causing property damage in excess of $6 billion. On Folly alone, some 300 houses either were destroyed or suffered extensive damage. But the rebuilding began almost immediately. With beach renourishment programs going full blast and new homes visible on many corners, property values on Folly zoomed upward for the first time in decades. Expensive homes were being constructed at the same time some small, older homes were being shut down for good.

The building of Folly Beach County Park for additional public access and completion of the new pier have added to the sense of rebirth for Folly, and the island's traditional sense of acceptance—for everyone from millionaires to surfers to members of the gay and lesbian communities—has assured a bustling, vital mix heading toward the new century.

How to Get There

Folly Island is about 10 miles south of Charleston. From downtown Charleston, take the four-lane expressway (SC 30) from Calhoun Street to SC 171, which crosses James Island leading to Folly. The trip usually takes about twenty minutes, a little longer during the morning and afternoon rush hours.

Where to Stay

Many visitors to Folly are day-trippers, and the beach is well suited for them. But for those who want to spend a night or more, there is a mix of accommodations ranging from expensive private homes that can be rented for a weekend or by the week, to small apartments and rooms. There are growing numbers of condominium units at Folly, and their construction has, in at least a few instances, resulted in blocking beach views to second-row residents and rental units. Such is the price of "progress," apparently. Nonetheless, there are several rental agencies located in the located in the business area as visitors drive on to the island.

In addition, there is a 132-room, six-story Holiday Inn, which is adjacent to the pier overlooking the Atlantic. At high tide, guests can look just about straight down from their balcony to the water.

Where to Eat

There are no chain restaurants on Folly, but there are several small, privately owned and operated restaurants serving a variety of beach food, fried and grilled, including a few perhaps unexpected dishes such as blackwater gumbo and grouper fingers. Several dining establishments can be found around the bridges over creeks on the causeway leading to Folly. One of the best-known and oldest is Bowens Island Restaurant, about a mile from Folly off 171 (look for the sign on the right before getting to the bridge to the beach), serving fried seafood in a building that seems to have successfully resisted modernization over the decades. That's putting it charitably.

Bowens Island is a classic of its own. Just getting there is a trip—literally, over a bumpy dirt road that leaves first-time visitors believing they're going the wrong way. The rather off-putting block structure is decorated—make that filled—with the graffiti of decades of drawings, numbers, names, and such. The interior is not so much decorated as stuffed with old TVs, a jukebox, a beauty shop dryer and, well, assorted junk. But, since the end of World War II, this restaurant has been serving up good seafood to locals and savvy visitors. The menu is fried shrimp, crabs, fish, stew, you-name-it. The seating is decidedly not fancy, the dress as casual as can be. It's not for everyone, perhaps, but most who stop here swear by the experience. It's open only for dinner. Don't worry about tipping the maitre d'.

Most of the in-town restaurants can be found close to the traffic light. One of them, the Seashell, has been in business for about five years, but there's been a restaurant at its central location for much longer. It's a good place to check out for a full breakfast and to get caught up on all the island's gossip from residents who frequently stop by. The new pier also has a restaurant where customers can sit inside or out and watch the beach while munching on a shrimp sandwich and French fries.

If you'd rather stay at home, there are small groceries on the island and large supermarkets a few miles away on James Island. Several establishments selling freshly caught shrimp ready for cooking and eating are easily found along the creeks.

What to Do

Gershwin wrote the lines, "Summertime, and the livin' is easy." So when it's summertime, head for the beach. Rental units have their own access, of course, but for everyone else there are lots of ways to enjoy the pleasures of the beach at Folly. The nicest access is located at the County Park at the western end of the island. To get there, turn right on Ashley Avenue and drive until you run out of road. (By the way, the DuBose Heyward home is at 712 Ashley, on the second row, on the way to County Park. It's not open to the public, however, and sometimes when the fence is closed it's not even visible to the public.)

The park, operated by Charleston County, is inviting. It has dressing areas, showers, restrooms, picnic areas, a snack bar, sheltered facilities, boardwalk ramps to the beach, beach equipment rentals, lifeguards, and lots of parking. There's a free public boat landing nearby, too.

There's 4,000 feet of beach in the park and another 2,000 feet of frontage on the Folly River. Or at least there was before a late 1990s storm blew way the lower half of the park, causing county officials to close off a number of parking areas until the damage could be repaired. Admission is only an inexpensive daily parking fee. Expect big crowds in midsummer when the park can fill up very early in the morning.

Scattered throughout the length of Folly are many small access areas with parking lots for a few vehicles and ramps leading to the beach. Several, such as the Folly Beach Park at Ashley and 4th Streets, have restrooms and changing areas. During the busy season, though, count on driving up and down the streets to locate an empty place. And when you find one, be sure to follow the posted instructions about parking limitations and beach rules. Public parking is allowed between 6 A.M. and 10 P.M.

The Folly Pier, in the center of the island adjacent to the Holiday Inn, was constructed in 1995 following two earlier piers. Twenty-five feet wide and extending 1,050 feet into the Atlantic, it is a landmark up and down the beach. Fishing is permitted (you can pay the appropriate fees in the concession shop at the pier), and sightseers can stroll its length for free. There are some picnic tables at the end and places to stop and sit to enjoy the view throughout its length.

The narrow "washout" zone near the northern (eastern) tip of Folly is the place to go for surfing. And sight-surfing. Depending on the condition of the water, there will be a crowd of surfers with their boards riding the waves or waiting patiently for the right wave to arrive. Parking is permitted along the washout zone. There are limits on where and when surfing is permitted. No surfing is allowed within 200 feet of the pier and in summer between the hours of 10 A.M. and 6 P.M. except at the washout.

Be aware of posted signs designating no-parking zones. Island police are sure to ticket you, especially in the busy summer months. There are also rules against walking on the dunes, having unleashed animals on the beach, and littering. The fines are $200 and the laws are enforced. Heed the signs pointing out no-swimming zones, too; The water can be very rough and dangerous even to experienced swimmers.

Sunbathing, despite the health risks, remains one of the favorite pastimes. It is practiced on decks, porches, or beaches. The occasional topless (female) sunbather can be seen, also, and while it's against the law, some discreet nudity seems to escape the attention of law enforcement officers around here.

To the north of the washout zone, the Morris Island lighthouse can be glimpsed. There's no land access, however: it's too far out at sea.

Churchgoers will find Our Lady of Good Counsel Catholic Church, Folly Beach Baptist Church, and Folly Beach United Methodist Church all with Sunday services. Other denominations have churches on nearby James Island and in Charleston. If you need to mail a letter, there's a post office on Folly, and there's also a branch of the county public library just in case you forgot to bring a book.

Shopping

It would be folly to expect high-end shopping areas here. The stores that cluster around the two block business district sell almost exclusively equipment and clothing and trinkets designed for beach use—hats, swimsuits, Frisbees, dark glasses, surf boards, towels, sandals, fishing tackle, and the like. McKelvin's Surf Shop, which opened in 1965, moved in the early 1980s, and enlarged after Hugo hit in 1989, long has been the mecca for East Coast surfers. It's worth a visit just to soak up the atmosphere. If you're looking for Armani, Gucci, Ralph Lauren, and their friends, however, remember they live in Charleston and Kiawah, not Folly.

There are gas stations on the island. And on James Island, between Folly Beach and Charleston and minutes from the beach, there are several shopping centers with fast-food restaurants, drive-by doctors, K-Marts, and movie theaters.

What to Wear

Folly is a very casual beach, and beachwear is acceptable everywhere, though there are restaurants that do require shirts and sandals. Heading into town, shirts and shoes are a necessity.

When to Go

It doesn't take a rocket scientist to figure out that Folly is at its most crowded in June, July, and August, when many people are taking vacations. Everything is open, everything is crowded, and prices are at their highest. Weekends are busiest, naturally, and the clamor for space is at its peak. Temperatures also are at their peak. The thermometer is usually into the 90s, and afternoon temperatures can and do rise over 100 from time to time. Usually, there's an ocean breeze to ease the pain, but if you don't like your beaches hot, avoid Folly in the summer.

Spring and fall are often delightful times to visit. Air temperatures moderate a bit and the water temperatures are still very comfortable. Best of all, the crowds are smaller and access is easier to come by. In the brief winter months of December, January, and February, there can be nice, sunny days for beach-walking, and, of course surfers in wet suits can be spotted, too. Temperatures occasionally hit 70 degrees just days after near-freezing temperatures. A number of the shops and restaurants are closed, however. Rates are at their cheapest for overnight and weekly rentals, and your accommodation choices will be unlimited during the winter season.

Five

Kiawah Island

Back around 1690, just a few years after the first permanent English settlement up the road a few miles near present-day Charleston, the English Lords Proprietors—the creators of Carolina—gave the Kiawah Indians an assortment of cloth, beads, and metal for the 10,000-acre island that now takes its name from that tribe. And you thought Manhattan was a steal?

Of course, for most of the next three hundred years, Kiawah (pronounced KEE-a-wah) was hardly a household name, even if George Gershwin did write an opera that sort of mentioned it. There were no championship golf courses. No fabulous, multi-million dollar homes. No tennis center. In fact, there weren't even any paved roads. That was then.

Now, fresh into the new millennium, Kiawah Island Resorts—a private, gated, semitropical barrier-island community—has emerged as one of the most famous of all resorts along the East Coast, ranked among the best beach resorts in the United States by several national magazines. It is a magnet for golfers who want to play the five lush courses where some of the world's finest golfers have teed off. It boasts ten miles of beautiful, secluded, shell-rich beaches and a series of atmospheric, moss-draped marshes and lagoons. There is an extensive system of tennis courts that host world-class tournaments. The island's development is consciously designed to blend into the fragile coastal ecosystem (no high-rises allowed). Kiawah Resorts is prepared to provide among the more luxurious and fairly expensive experiences to be found for vacationers to the South Carolina coast.

Kiawah's natural beauty can take even the wary by surprise. The centuries-old maritime forest—large growths of live oaks, tall pines, magnolias, and palmettos—is host to an extraordinary assortment of wildlife, not even counting the mosquitoes. The island claims to account for more than 170 species of birds (bring your binoculars), eighteen different mammals including lots of deer and raccoons (keep your garbage lids securely closed), and 30 varieties of reptiles and amphibians, including the alligators that occasionally can temporarily disrupt or rearrange a golf game. Not to fear; the gators do not chase golfers around the course. On the other hand, if you hit a shot into the water, it might be a wise decision to use another ball rather than charging into an alligator's living room. Experts say you're perfectly safe as long as you and the alligator are separated by at least 60 feet. If you're slow, better make it 90 feet.

Kiawah Island is usually thought of as one of the Charleston area beaches because of its proximity to the city, a matter of only 21 miles, or less than one hour from the airport. But Kiawah has quite a different character—and development—than the Charleston beaches to the north: Folly Beach, Sullivan's Island, and the Isle of Palms. For one, Kiawah Island Resorts is private. There is a guarded entrance gate, and the curious will be turned away. Of course, residents and visitors with reservations are invited, and others with specific missions—such as checking out real estate bargains here—also will receive limited-admission passes. Day-trippers may use the Kiawah Beachwalker County Park, operated by Charleston County Park and Recreation Commission, which offers the only public beach access on the island. It's a beautiful stretch of beach, but it's limited by private ownership of the rest of the island.

In the well-manicured resort, with its electric-cart lifestyle, there are private homes and villas and an inn, all of which may be rented by visitors year-round. On the part of the island that requires admission through yet another gate are private residences and some magnificent palaces that would fit comfortably into the landscape at Newport, Rhode Island (the green at Kiawah is not all found on the golf courses). If you'd like an upscale beach vacation, Kiawah fits the bill very nicely. It has plenty of facilities to entice families and lots of activities for the more serious-minded who want to take care of business on the golf course.

And while it might seem probable that a golfer (maybe named Nicklaus?) founded the island, that's not quite the case. The earliest known settlers were the Indians, who survived comfortably in the warm climate hunting and fishing on these rich lands until the arrival of the English in the 1690s. Soon thereafter, the Indians began disappearing as landowners sent African slaves to the island to tend their free-ranging cattle. By 1737, a wealthy planter and merchant named John Stanyarne had acquired the island and began a move away from agriculture to indigo, which proved so profitable it quickly became known as "blue gold." Kiawah remained in the possession of Stanyarne's descendants well into the next century.

Cotton became the king crop on Kiawah in the nineteenth century, a crop which required intensive slave labor on the large plantations. The Civil War brought dramatic change to Kiawah, however. With the capture of nearby Hilton Head Island by Union soldiers in 1862, slaves were removed from the island in anticipation of an eventual advance against Charleston (which did occur later in the war). There was considerable property damage as a result of the war's ravages. By 1900, though, the island was again under just one owner and claimed a total population of less than a hundred, including a scattering of black tenant farmers.

Kiawah's seclusion was broken by the establishment of daily passenger and freight service on a boat connecting the island to Charleston around 1900 (and continuing well past the destructive 1911 hurricane). With stops, the journey required four hours. That boat trip was memorialized by the Charleston writer DuBose Heyward in his 1925 novel *Porgy*. And it was later incorporated into George Gershwin's opera *Porgy and Bess,* based on Heyward's work. (In the opera's second act, the residents of Catfish Row in Charleston head off by boat for a picnic at "Kittiwah" Island. Heyward had worked for a year with a Charleston steamship company, and no doubt was familiar with the operation of the service back and forth to Kiawah when he sat down to write *Porgy.*)

In the early 1950s, Kiawah was sold and used primarily for logging purposes and a family retreat. But when a bridge was built connecting it to Johns Island, which had roads leading into Charleston, the development of Kiawah as a visitor destination was assured. There have been a variety of owners (including an investment group from the oil-rich Kuwaiti kingdom) in the second half of the twentieth century, and the island's amenities have been sold several times. In recent years, however, owner stability has led to a series of renovations and improvements, placing Kiawah at its current eminence as a popular upscale golf and tennis beach resort and a centerpiece in the growth of nature-based tourism.

FOR INFORMATION on Kiawah Island Resorts, call (800) 654-2924 or (843) 768-2121, or go to the resort's website, www.kiawahresort.com.

Getting There

Kiawah Island is 21 miles from Charleston. From the Charleston International Airport, 33 miles away, the driving time is usually no more than about 45 minutes. The island's closeness to Charleston means that it's easy for visitors to Kiawah to drive into the city for a day or night to savor the pleasures of America's friendliest city and one of its most historically fascinating, too. The Charleston Executive Airport provides landing space for private planes; it's only 9 miles from Kiawah.

If you're driving into Charleston from either north or south or coming from the city, there are plenty of clearly marked signs pointing the way to Kiawah. Arriving from the north on Interstate 26, take I-526 West to US Highway 17 South for about 5 miles, then turn left at Main Road and continue following the signs. Coming north to Charleston on US Highway 17, just look for the sign to Kiawah at Main Road. It will be a right-hand turn.

Main Road leading into Kiawah—it becomes Bohicket Road after crossing Highway 700—is mostly two lanes, so traffic can be a little slow here especially during the morning and afternoon rush hours (yes, even for island paradises, there can be traffic snarls, although at its worst, Bohicket Road is no Malfunction Junction). Highway 700 also provides access back to Charleston through busy, commercial James Island.

Once you arrive at the Kiawah gate, you'll get a map and easy instructions for getting around the resort.

Getting Oriented

There are two parts of Kiawah Island Resorts—West Beach Village and East Beach Village—and the twain do indeed meet, connected by the Kiawah Island Parkway. There's a shuttle service for visitors to get around, and cars or bikes are handy, too. The island has nearly thirty miles of landscaped jogging trails, so it's possible to do your getting around on foot if you wish. You can also walk on the beach from one area to the other.

The two villages are where visitors will find accommodations, restaurants and activities, including access to golf and tennis. However, the Ocean Beach Course, Kiawah's most famous eighteen holes, and beautiful Osprey Point Course are reached through another security gate on the Parkway leading to the eastern, less developed end of the island. That's where the large, private residences may be found, but only residents and their guests and registered golfers are allowed into this area.

West Beach Village, which is reached immediately after passing through the first security gate, is the location of the Kiawah Island Inn and a variety of villas, restaurants, shops, and tennis courts. It is the older of the developed sections of the island. It also the location of the Cougar Point Golf Course.

East Beach Village offers homes and villas for rental along with the Kiawah Town Center with restaurants, a market and the twenty-one-acre

Night Heron Park for nature-connected activities. East Beach Village also is the site for the island's largest conference center, which can accommodate up to eight hundred persons, and it is closest to the Turtle Point Golf Course.

Day-trippers or anyone wishing to bypass Kiawah's entrance gate can drive directly to Beachwalker County Park at Kiawah's western end for a delightful beach experience. The sand is as white here as it is in front of Kiawah Resort's expensive villas. The county maintains the beach with a parking area, picnic area, dressing space, restrooms, a snack bar, and outside showers. There's a small admission charge in summer.

When to Go

When do you get in the mood to play some golf at a course so attractively laid out it will knock your knickers off? Winter, when the temperatures are mild? Spring or fall, when the climate is warm with less chance of rain? Or summer, when the sun-baked course and sea breezes offer different sorts of challenges? There's really no bad time to head for Kiawah, whether you're planning to golf, play tennis, or just enjoy the beaches. If it's swimming you're after, however, you might want a rubber suit during the winter months, when it's just nervy Canadians who seem to want to frolic in the very chilly Atlantic Ocean.

The average temperature in January on Kiawah is 59 degrees. By April it's 76. In July and August, the average goes up to 86. By November it's down to 69. What that means, of course, is that it gets very hot in the summer and not terribly cold for too long a period in the winter months. Expect high temperatures and humidity June through September; readings up to 100 are not routine but they're not unexpected, either. There's usually a breeze on the beaches to help out. Late afternoon thunderstorms occur regularly, too, but they seldom last long.

Spring and summer are the best times for a visit, according to many vacationers. The humidity drops, making the outdoor activities even more pleasurable. Golf and tennis are a delight, and so are the beaches (the ocean is warm enough for most folks to go swimming from May through October). Of course just walking along Kiawah's glorious white sand beaches is a treat no matter the time of year. In winter, you'll want sweaters and hats. That breeze that seemed so refreshing in July can prove downright cold in January. Even so, most days at Kiawah December through March are just fine for your outdoor activity of choice.

Accommodations

There are three options for anyone planning a stay at Kiawah Island Resorts: the Kiawah Island Inn, a villa in one of fifteen complexes, or a private home. There aren't many of the latter for rental, and they can be expensive (that is, unless you don't consider $800 a night on the pricey side), though you can find less expensive—but they provide the most exclusive and luxurious experience on an island that lives by the upscale.

The green-shirted, straw-hatted members of the staff who greet you at the Kiawah Island Inn help set the tone for the resort: Relax. We'll take care of you and help you do whatever you want. The inn recently got a much-needed facelift, though it has some rooms on the small side and has been around ever since the resort got started more than three decades ago. (Construction is nearing completion on a new hotel in the resort.) The existing 150 inn rooms in four separate groupings have balconies with views; you'll pay more for the ocean views, of course. The usual amenities are included: cable television, refrigerators, hair dryers, and such. The inn complex has three pools, three restaurants, an oceanfront lounge, and a summer-season bar. Everything is within a short walk—especially the beach.

Guests at the inn—or any of the villas—receive resort benefits, too. These include a free hour of tennis, substantial discounts for a round of golf, special kid's events, and preferred access to all of the recreation programs. Ask for details when you make a reservation.

The villas are spread out over the East Beach and West Beach areas. To register and pick up your keys when you arrive for a villa stay, head for the Town Center in East Beach Village.

Some of the villas face the ocean, some are situated on a lagoon or in a woodsy area, while others bump up to tennis courts. The location is your choice. Prices are highest for oceanfront villas and go up depending on how many bedrooms you may require. For the least expensive villas, look for locations in the woods or on lagoons away from the beach.

For villas with the best oceanfront views, try Duneside, Seascape, Marriner's Watch, Shipwatch, or Windswept. The latter is just about as much of a high-rise as you'll find at Kiawah, but the views from all can be pretty spectacular. The villas offer one-, two-, and three-bedroom units.

Other villas around the island come with different views. Turtle Point villas, for instance, are two- and three-bedroom units close to the Turtle Point course and tennis. They are on a lagoon but have easy beach access. Parkside has two- and three-bedroom flats and townhomes on a lagoon five minutes away from the beach. Sparrow Pond features single-family cottages in a secluded wood a few minutes' walk from the shops at West Beach. And Tennis Club villas has units with screened porches facing the East Beach Tennis Club, perfect for racket fans. The beach is a ten-minute walk away.

Accommodations in the resort are limited. And on busy summer weekends, especially, it can be difficult to find just what you want at the last minute.

Early reservations are recommended, particularly if you want one of the popular oceanfront villas. Calling in January or February usually will get you what you prefer for midsummer weeks. Be aware that spring and fall are very popular, along with holidays, and accommodations can be hard to get as well as more costly. Most of the villas and homes rent for a minimum one-week period in the summer season (and some out of season, too). Rooms at the inn can be rented for shorter periods. When championship golf or tennis matches are being held at Kiawah, rooms will be in very short supply and you may wind up having to stay off the island.

Rates for double rooms in the inn vary from about $120 to $275 a night depending on the season. A two-bedroom villa with an ocean view rents for anywhere from about $1,300 to more than $3,000 per week, again depending on the season. There are specially priced golf and tennis packages available; be sure to ask.

Dining

Kiawah Island Resorts offers a variety of dining experiences. You can eat cheaply picnic-style or you can drop the big bucks at a fine meal in one of several nice restaurants, though visitors seeking the highest levels of cuisine shouldn't miss driving in to Charleston.

The highly rated dining room at the Osprey Point Clubhouse and the Atlantic Room in the Kiawah Inn are the resort's top dining locations. Opened in 1997, the Osprey Point facilities in East Beach village are done in a plantation-style setting with excellent views whether you're dining upscale upstairs or casually on the covered decks and terraces. The restaurant serves breakfast, lunch, and dinner and is open to resort guests and property owners.

Close to the ocean and shaded by live oaks, the Atlantic Room in West Beach Village serves a buffet breakfast as well as dinner. The menu at both restaurants includes lots of fresh seafood (you weren't expecting anything else, were you?) with standard American dishes. Dinner entrées at both restaurants range from $12 to $28. Dress is appropriate, which means jackets and ties aren't necessary, but shoes and shirts are. Actually, for dinner especially, many guests do wear a jacket and evening attire. It depends on how dressed up you feel like getting.

If you don't feel like getting dressed up at all, however, there are options for you, too. The Sundancer Bar and Grill serves up hamburgers and the like from a beachside location in West Beach Village (summers only). Also, the West Beach Café has a little more substantial fare, including seafood.

In East Beach village, The Village Bistro offers casual dining just right for families (young kids welcome) with dishes including pastas, steaks, and

The Pete Dye-designed Kiawah Island Ocean Course at Kiawah Island received international attention in1991 when it was host to the Ryder Cup. The course also was host to the World Cup of Golf in 1997. (Photograph courtesy of the South Carolina Department of Parks, Recreation & Tourism)

seafood. Also, the clubhouse at the Ocean Course serves three meals daily in a casual setting suited to the links. The ocean view from the veranda is a special treat after a round of golf.

If you're staying in a villa and want to replenish your food supplies, the Market at Town Center in East Beach Village has a selection of groceries. If you are looking for supermarket quantity and prices, however, you'll have to head back to Bohicket Road and Highway 700, where there are several choices. Or stop there on the way to Kiawah and carry your supplies to the island with you. (A word of warning; if it's important to you to save a quarter on the price of a six-pack of beer, Kiawah may not be your vacation nirvana.)

Golf

Not everybody who comes to Kiawah is drawn by the golf, but for those who are, this is one of America's great golf destinations. Robert Redford apparently thought so too. This is where much of the year-2000 film he directed, *The Legend of Bagger Vance,* starring Will Smith and Matt Damon, was shot, though the climactic hole in that movie was specially constructed for the purpose and, as a result, can't be seen by visitors.

There are five courses in the resort. They were designed by Jack Nicklaus, Tom Fazio, Gary Player, Clyde Johnston, and Pete Dye. That's world-class. Or what Southerners would call high cotton. It hardly gets any better. Golfers would be hard-pressed to find such a quintet of championship courses all on the same 10,000-acre island. Fortunately, they don't have to. All they have to do is come—bring your equipment or rent—and enjoy it. And tens of thousands do every year.

Kiawah is annually rated by *Golf Digest* as one of the nation's top five golf resorts. *Condé Nast Traveler* magazine ranks it among the top fifty golf resorts worldwide. Just about all of the best golfers in the world have challenged these courses, which have hosted the Ryder Cup and PGA Cup Matches as well as numerous Carolinas amateur and professional events.

The Ocean Course, designed by Dye, opened just months before the 1991 Ryder Cup matches. All eighteen holes offer panoramic views of the Atlantic Ocean, but don't get too caught up in the views. *Golf Digest* also calls it "America's toughest resort course." Ten of the holes play directly along the beach, where the winds can make every stroke treacherous. The par 72 course stretches 7,371 yards from the gold tees and 5,372 from the forward tees. The clubhouse has restaurant, bar, pro shop, and locker rooms.

Osprey Point course is eighteen holes, par 72 covering 6,678 yards from the gold tees and 5,122 yards from the forward tees. Designed by Fazio, it makes elegant use of a landscape that includes saltwater marshes, live oak forests, and four large natural lakes affording surprising variety in shot-making. The clubhouse has restaurant, bar, lounge, pro shop, and locker rooms.

Turtle Point Course was designed by Nicklaus and hosted the 1990 PGA Cup matches on its eighteen-hole, par 72 layout. With its combination of length and accuracy and low profile, it has been the site of many regional championships. Most appealing is a three-hole stretch woven through rolling sand dunes directly fronting the Atlantic. The course is 6,925 yards from the gold tees and 5,285 from the forward tees. The clubhouse has a snack bar and pro shop.

Cougar Point course opened in 1996 designed by Player. Its eighteen-hole, par 72 layout stretches 6,808 yards from the gold tees to 4,722 yards from the green tees. The course plays along stunning tidal marshes with views of the historic Kiawah River. Constructed on the site of the former Marsh Point Golf Course, this completely new course has a halfway house on the tenth hole and a pro shop.

Nearby but outside the Kiawah entrance gate is Oak Point, an eighteen-hole, par 72 course that Kiawah Resorts owns and guests also may use. Built on the grounds of an old indigo and cotton plantation, it plays along the

Kiawah River and around marshes and winding creeks. Referred to as a Scottish-American course, it is a test for novices and experienced players alike. Designed by Clyde Johnston, it covers 6,759 yards from the black tees to 4,484 from the red tees.

Greens fees are highest at the Ocean Course (over $200), but there's a good discount—up to $45—for resort guests. It's considerably less than half that to play Oak Point.

The resort offers private and group lessons for beginners and pros and offers arrangements for groups up to two hundred who want to play golf. Special packages and group rates are available throughout the year, too. If you want to play the Ocean Course at a certain time, it's a good idea to reserve a tee time before you get to the resort.

Tennis

It's okay if your name isn't Agassi or Navratilova or McEnroe or Evert. Kiawah's tennis courts are wide open to you. Just beware that some of the best in the world have played here before you.

The resort has been rated as high as third on *Tennis* magazine's list of the "Top 50 Greatest U.S. Tennis Resorts." And it draws lots of attention year-round. And here's a deal: Every guest at the resort is entitled to one free hour on the court each day. That doesn't come with a guarantee about quality of play, unfortunately. Nor does it discount time spent retrieving errant shots.

Kiawah has two comprehensive, fully stocked tennis complexes. Both have pro shops, rentals, apparel, and daily clinics. Private and group lessons are offered. The West Beach Tennis Club, open year-round, is just a short stroll from the Kiawah Inn. It features fourteen clay (composition) courts and two lighted Har-Tru courts. The East Beach Village Tennis Club near Town Center has nine clay (composition) courts (one lighted) and three hard courts (one lighted). The club is open seasonally. It also has a zoned practice court with ball machine and an automated retrieval system, just in case you hit an occasional line drive where you didn't intend it to go.

The resort's tennis program is structured to provide fun for all ages. Free clinics pair players of competitive abilities from spring until fall, and there are games pairing parents and their youngsters as well as games for the kids by themselves. In fact, if a youngster is old enough to walk and reasonably potty-trained, Kiawah's pros probably can get him started with a racket. The "Tiny Tots Program" takes kids as young as age four. Older kids can enroll in tennis camp and receive intensive training several hours a day.

Reservations are required to get on the courts; resort officials can handle the details as well as booking any special needs. Advance reservations for court time before getting to the resort are seldom necessary (unless your four-year-old has special nap times, perhaps).

Recreation

Even if you don't play golf and you don't play tennis, your Kiawah vacation will not be a bust. For starters, you've got nearly ten miles of some of the most beautiful beach you'll find anywhere along the Atlantic coast. Take a walk. You'll soon see why *National Geographic Traveler* magazine rates Kiawah among the five most romantic beaches in America. If you fancy shells, Kiawah is renowned for its appeal to collectors. There are lots of unusual shells to be found on these beaches, so get an early start in the morning and see what treasures have washed up.

Apart from beach strolls or jogs and shell-searching, there are a lot of outdoor activities featured at the resort. And they are designed for families together as well as all ages separately.

Because of the island's length, many visitors enjoy renting bicycles to get around. It's much faster than climbing into a car (no kidding) and more environmentally satisfying, too. You can get everywhere on the island on two wheels, because Kiawah has some thirty miles of special bike trails. Half-day, full-day, three-day, or weekly rentals are offered, and with the beach bikes and level terrain, you needn't fear changing gears. Helmets, child seats, tandems, and tow carts are available, too. Just ask.

Once you've decided how to get around, then where to go? Head for Night Heron Park in the East Beach Village. It's a popular destination point for many visitors to the island and gets a lot of repeaters as well. The nature center is staffed by knowledge naturalists year-round, and they'll be glad to show you the exhibits that allow you to see up close some of the island's inhabitants, including lizards, snakes, and turtles. You can touch some of them if you'd like, but you don't have to if you're squeamish.

From the center there are nature walks around the island, birding expeditions—there are nearly as many species of birds on Kiawah as visitors—kayaking on the Kiawah River or canoeing on the marsh (for novices or experienced paddlers), opportunities to study Kiawah's unique pond system, and night walks to observe the island's nocturnal critters. The latter is a lot of fun and highly recommended; it gives visitors a very different look at an environment that seems quite unusual when the sun goes down. Not all of these activities are offered year-round, but in summer the center is constantly in motion with one activity following another. It's a great place to hang out for kids and adults.

In addition, the park boasts a full-length basketball court, a swimming pool complex with a 25-meter junior Olympic pool (there are also pools at the

Kiawah Inn and East Beach Tennis Center), a soccer field, and places for cook-outs and even occasional summer concerts.

Especially for kids is Camp Kiawah, geared to ages three to eleven with supervised fun for a half day or full day. Programs for teenagers include late-night movies, basketball games, dances, and pool parties. These activities are scheduled in the summer and on holidays. Call ahead if you want to be certain specific programs are available.

By the way, there is not a spa on Kiawah, but there is a staff that offers some massage and therapeutic treatments for guests. The choices include Swedish massage, facelift massage, and foot reflexology, for those days when you're feeling in need of a little pampering. Check with the Kiawah Inn for reservations.

And finally, one cautionary note: mosquitoes and no-see-ums (they're hard to spot until they land on you and begin biting) accompany visitors on outdoor jaunts at Kiawah. Count on it and prepare with repellent or whatever works for you. If you forget to bring some, you'll find plenty at the resort stores.

Shopping

And speaking of stores, visitors don't have to leave Kiawah to find a variety of wares. If you're into shopping in a big way, however, head immediately for Charleston, 21 miles away. That's where the folks named Gucci, Rolex, Ralph Lauren, Saks, and their friends live. On Kiawah, you'll find some high-end merchandise but not the selection you'll encounter in Charleston.

Shops at the Kiawah Island Inn in West Beach Village offer a delightful assortment of fourteen establishments, featuring beach clothing—everything from shorts to towels to sweaters—to ice cream parlors. Everything here is casual, and the shops are open seven days a week. And at the Market in Town Center, East Beach Village, you'll find a smaller supply of clothing with sundries, newspapers, and the like. It's also open seven days a week.

Seabrook Island

FOR INFORMATION call (800) 845-2233 or (843) 768-5056, or go to www.seabrook.com.

• •

Seabrook is something of a little sister to Kiawah Island. Located just a few minutes from Kiawah down Bohicket Road and about 23 miles from Charleston, it offers some of the same features, landscape and pleasures as the much-larger Kiawah. It is a 2,200-acre upscale gated resort and private country club community with three miles of beach spread over ocean and inlet.

Residential and rental villas overlook the peaceful dunes of Seabrook Island.
(Photograph © 2001 Robert Clark)

Few of its rental villas, however, are actually on the ocean; many of the homes that front the Atlantic are private residences, and not all are open to seasonal vacationers (unless, of course, you're good friends with the owner, and if that's the case, congratulations on your good fortune and enjoy your stay). Seabrook also has a conference center accommodating groups up to three hundred. Participants stay at villas or homes around the island and hold their meetings at the center, at the southern end of Seabrook of the island where the Atlantic Ocean meets the North Edisto River Inlet.

This barrier island is beautifully maintained and designed to allow most of the development to fit comfortably and unobtrusively into the natural surroundings. The landscaping is lush with palmettos, oaks, pines, salt marshes, and wildflowers, and the habitat is rich in wildlife. There are more than 150 species of birds to be seen here, along with deer, raccoon, loggerhead turtles, and alligators. This is, however, a private resort, and only guests are invited to use the facilities, which include two golf courses, tennis courts, and opportunities for everything from biking to fishing to horseback riding.

Accommodations range from one to four bedrooms in the well-furnished villas and private homes. While the highest-priced have ocean views, the majority of the units have scenic vistas around the marshes, creeks, inlet, or fairways. Weekly prices for a two-bedroom villa range from about $500 to $1,700 depending on location and the time of year, with midsummer rates traditionally the highest. Very few units are available for daily rentals in summer, far more in the other seasons. And as elsewhere, spring and fall are becoming more popular with visitors, so expect rental prices to be edging upward. The resort has special packages for golfers, for honeymooners, and for holiday periods. Ask for details when you make a reservation.

When it's time to eat, Seabrook offers the Seaview Restaurant and Half Shell Lounge at the Conference Center. Bohicket Marina Village has restaurants, and so does the Village Center Market; both of those are just outside the security gate. For more dining options, Charleston is a relatively short drive away.

Seabrook has lots of recreational joys. In addition to strolling the beach, swimming, and shelling, visitors can cruise the marshes in a kayak or canoe, rent a motorboat, charter a deep-sea fishing boat—wahoo, king mackerel, amberjack and dolphin are the likely targets—or perhaps take parasailing lessons. There's an equestrian center offering lessons for kids and their parents.

The Seabrook Island Club has special kids' programs during summer months—with video games and ping-pong tables—and activities for teens, including pool parties, dances, and athletic competition. The club has a couple of swimming pools and a basketball court. Most guests have access to the club facilities, but be sure to ask when you're inquiring into reservations.

Golfers can tackle two challenging eighteen-hole courses on the island. The 6,910-yard Crooked Oaks course was designed by Robert Trent Jones, and the 6,805-yard Ocean Winds course was laid out by Willard Byrd. Both wind gracefully past tidal creeks and moss-draped oaks to make a round of golf an aesthetic delight. In addition, the packages allow golfers to visit other layouts, among them nearby Kiawah Resort's fabulous courses. And tennis players will be happy with the thirteen Har-Tru composition courts at the Seabrook Racquet Club, complete with pro shop and clinics for all ages.

Bohicket Marina Village, which you will come to shortly before arriving at Seabrook's security gate, has a full-service marina. If you're arriving by boat, this is the place to drop anchor. The marina also has shops and eating establishments and is the place to go for most of the beach activity rentals. If you're going to Seabrook for vacation, stop at the Village Center just before getting to the gated entrance to check in and get your keys and directions.

Six

Edisto Island

If not for a bunch of far-thinking Indians who decided the virtues of tourism were overrated, Edisto Island might have been the site of the first permanent English settlement in South Carolina. Back in 1666, four years before the founding of the colony at what would become Charleston, an English explorer by the name of Robert Sandford dropped anchor at Edisto Island, which was then just another piece of the New World as yet unnamed by the English. Sandford and his small band met the Indians on the island, who called themselves Edistows. It would be wonderful to know how that meeting went, the explorers captivated by the strange natives, and the natives probably pretty much amazed by the foreigners.

In any event, after a friendly initial meeting, the Edistows began to sense something might not work out to their benefit. Hence, with classic misdirection, they pointed Sandford a little farther north where, the explorer was assured, the natives were not only warm and friendly but also generous and peaceful. Sandford reported back to his superiors in England, and four years later settlers sailed into current-day Charleston, a few miles north of Edisto Island. The story doesn't have an especially happy ending, at least for the Edistows. A few years later, this mellow tribe seems to have dropped off the island, possibly after clashes with more warlike tribes, and they make few appearances in the history books after that.

Another figure on Edisto Island about 250 years later had a rather unhappy ending, too. His name was John McConkey, and in the late nineteenth century he was a prominent landowner. At the time the beach was known as McConkey Beach. In 1915, however, McConkey was "cruelly murdered," according to the inscription on his tombstone on the island. The assailant was never caught, and the murder remains unsolved to this day. McConkey not only lost his life, but his name on the beach, too. Since the early 1920s, it's been known as Edisto Beach, once quite isolated and inaccessible, now a quiet and lovely beach, popular with families. Longtime residents and vacationers who have returned year after year for generations speak in hushed tones about "their" island, fearful its character may be changed if there is yet another invasion of visitors from far away.

Outside of the state's borders, Edisto may be the least-known of South Carolina's beaches. It does not have full-time marketing and public relations employees who "sell" the island in national magazines. It has no high-rise hotels and motels. In fact, it has no hotels or motels at all. There's virtually nothing of convention facilities. The beach is dotted with small private homes and summer houses, many of which are wonderfully weathered with age. Their look typifies the feel here: casual and comfortable, sort of like a favorite old shoe. Edisto isn't particularly convenient to get to, at least in the sense that there is no interstate highway which ends in the surf—thank goodness. Like better-known Pawleys Island to the north, to which it is sometimes compared, Edisto has sternly resisted the siren call of development. That has given this beach a very special charm found at few places along the South Carolina coast. If you like the idea of small-town, you'll probably like the reality of Edisto.

Visitors first should know there is an Edisto Beach and an Edisto Island. The former is a part of the latter, and they are linked. Edisto Island is a town located on Edisto Island, with a series of marshes and creeks crisscrossing both. Edisto Beach is a small community, except in summer when its numbers swell—comparatively speaking—with visitors. These are not, however, urban areas we're talking about, but instead a few restaurants, some shops, and one golf course development with low-rise condominiums. The sleek, modern, golf-cart lifestyle that works at other beaches on the coast is noticeably absent here, and hardly anyone seems upset about it.

Edisto Island, with its fifty-five square miles, has a rich history that goes back long before Sandford and his Englishmen arrived in the seventeenth century. Indians were the earliest occupants, and they occasionally ran into the Spanish, who are believed briefly to have located a mission nearby. The Spanish called the island "Oristo," probably a corruption of what they understood to be the name of the local tribe.

The island was purchased from the Indians in 1674—most likely another bad deal for the locals—and English settlers arrived soon after. They were kept busy fending off Spanish raiders for a few years before settling into a profitable agricultural existence in the early years of the eighteenth century.

Seafood harvested from local waterways plays an important part in the coastal economy and provides a treat for the lowcountry table. (Photograph © 2001 Robert Clark)

The introduction of indigo into the economy made planters rich. A century later cotton was the money crop, and the planters grew richer, importing ever-larger numbers of slaves to work the fields.

The Edisto beaches were popular with visitors in the early nineteenth century, when the island claimed 250 white inhabitants and some 3,000 slaves. The beach at Edingsville—named after one of the sea island cotton planters—became an attraction in the years before the Civil War. There were dozens of cottages and even a boardwalk around 1820. Use of the beach gradually declined in use after the war, and in 1893, a fierce hurricane leveled the homes and the island. The original Edingsville no longer exists, though fishermen and hunters for some years found artifacts from the destroyed cottages in the marshes behind modern-day Edisto Beach.

The Civil War brought dramatic changes. In 1862, Union soldiers arrived in the South Carolina sea islands, and white plantation owners fled, taking their slaves in some cases, abandoning them in others. Federal regiments throughout the war occupied Edisto Island, and when the hostilities ended, a way of life for the cotton planters had disappeared—along with their slaves and wealth.

The island's agricultural economy was shattered, and the reconstruction of the land was hampered in the postwar years by a series of hurricanes and, even later, by the boll weevil's destructive path through cotton. Isolated, accessible only by boat, of unprepossessing economic worth, Edisto languished.

The beach as it is known today was not developed until the early 1920s, and it grew very slowly. The few cottages built on the beach were constructed without benefit of roads or electricity. One local historian says the island's isolation in the Prohibition era of the 1920s led to a large-scale illegal whiskey operation near the creeks that crisscross the area.

The Depression and World War II imposed additional limits on expansion, though a state park was opened in the late 1930s, built by the Roosevelt administration's Civilian Conservation Corps. The modern era began after World War II, though growth was slow when compared to the boom at the Grand Strand, for example. The beach always retained its family flavor, and the lack of major highway access and determination to resist development helped to ensure that growth would be slow. Air conditioning in homes here, for instance, arrived much later than at many other beaches.

Word of mouth has long been an ally of this jewel of a beach, so be careful about underestimating its popularity with those in the know. Just because it's a small dot on the map next to a place like Myrtle Beach, don't plan on showing up on a summer weekend without reservations and expect to find a beachfront home waiting for you. It's always possible—shrimp, after all, might indeed whistle some day—but don't bet your vacation on it.

Getting There

Arriving at Edisto is a lot easier than it used to be, though it takes a bit of a circuitous journey to arrive at your destination. Not to worry; take your time and enjoy the spectacular scenery and lowcountry vistas along the way. It makes for a memorable trip. Edisto Beach is about 45 miles south of Charleston and the same distance to the southeast from Walterboro. And there's a story behind that situation which might point up the sense of independence that hangs over the island like summer humidity.

Edisto Beach used to be a part of Charleston County. In 1860, when South Carolina was debating whether to leave the Union, the delegate from Edisto stood up and shouted that if the state wouldn't vote to secede, Edisto for sure would. Fast-forward a hundred years later and Edisto voted once again to secede: this time from Charleston County. Residents felt they weren't getting enough attention and services from populous Charleston, so they voted to hook up with Colleton County, whose county seat happens to be in Walterboro. Hence, it's interesting to note—for history's sake, if nothing else—that Edisto is about the same distance from both cities.

Arriving by car, whether you come from the north or the south, it makes little difference because there's only one roadway. It's called Highway 174.

If you're traveling on Interstate 95, take the Walterboro exit (US 64). Follow 64 through Walterboro for 15 miles to its intersection with US 17 at the small town of Jacksonboro. Turn left on 17 heading toward Charleston, and after about 6 miles begin looking for the right turn on 174. It's marked clearly. Two-lane Highway 174 leads directly—more or less—to Edisto Beach, approximately 25 miles away. The trip passes several historic spots, and Spanish moss hangs atmospherically over parts of the roadway.

If you're coming from Charleston follow the signs to US 17 South (in the direction of Savannah) and stay on it until you get to the 174 turn. Or, if you'd like to pay a visit to Hollywood—no kidding—before you get to Edisto, turn left on State Highway 162 at Rantowles and follow it through the small town of Hollywood to its ultimate intersection with 174. There's not a movie studio in sight in this little town, but the shrimp here are a lot fresher than you'll find in Tinseltown. There's not much difference in driving time either way, but at the least you can tell your friends you got a glimpse of Hollywood in South Carolina.

Highway 174 cuts right through Edisto Island to Edisto Beach, so don't worry about getting lost. The travel time from Charleston International Airport is about an hour or so. There's not an airstrip for private planes around Edisto, but there is a public marina on the island, so you can arrive by boat.

Getting Oriented

Leave your car's electronic navigational device at home for this trip. Edisto Beach is small, easy to get around on, and exceedingly difficult to get lost on. The congestion that plagues Hilton Head and Myrtle Beach does not exist here. Highway 174 brings you on to the northern end of the island and dead-ends at Palmetto Boulevard, which parallels the beach as it runs down to the southern end of Edisto Beach.

The beach curves away from the Atlantic Ocean at its southern end, so that the last few blocks have homes that front St. Helena Sound. As you drive down Palmetto Boulevard, beachfront homes will be on the left, second row and inland on the right. The golf course and condo development is reached by turning right on Lybrand Street (just past the middle of the island), which will take you along the back side (or creek side) of Edisto Beach.

Edisto Beach State Park is located off 174 just before it reaches the beach at Palmetto Boulevard. The signs are easy to follow.

Traffic moves in both directions on all of the beach roads except for a few in the condo development. The speed limits are posted and are strictly enforced. There are lots of people walking and biking in the summer months, so take it easy when you're driving. If you're on foot along Palmetto Boulevard, keep an eye out for traffic moving faster than it should. If you're on two wheels, stick to the new bike paths.

Climate

As with all the beaches along South Carolina's coast, summer is prime time. The weather is hot—most often 90 degrees and above—and you'll know you're in tropical conditions. The sea breezes can make the days a little pleasanter, but expect to get hot. The nights cool off only a little, and they are usually pretty sticky, too. If you don't use air conditioning, a fan would be a welcome accompaniment to sleep. It does rain from time to time, and some big thunderstorms can roll across the beach, but as a rule they come in the late afternoon when the heats builds up and usually disappear by dinnertime. Very few week-long vacations are ruined because it rains all the time.

As with other beaches also, the spring and fall are delightful times to visit since the weather is a little milder and what passes for crowds at Edisto have thinned out. The ocean water is quite comfortable for swimming well into the fall months. Before May, however, it's too chilly for most folks.

The winter months are free of really cold weather (although natives can tell you it does get pretty darned chilly); even so, you can expect to encounter some gloriously sunny, mild days in January, February, and March. You can also run into some days when the wind blows and the sun doesn't show and you're very grateful for three layers of sweaters. Fear not: the sun returns quickly, and even if you can't get in the water, beachcombing remains a year-round delight, and so is fossil-hunting. The ocean is a free treat, no matter the time of year.

Accommodations

There are not so many choices as to befuddle the vacationer on Edisto. For starters, there's not a hotel or motel at this beach. Many travelers can't imagine staying anywhere but in one of the older beachfront or second row homes that have long been landmarks at this beach. Nearly all of those homes have at least three bedrooms, and some will be able to accommodate up to fourteen or eighteen, perfect for groups of families who might want to stay together and share the costs. These cottages tend to be one- or two-story homes, and they come furnished with kitchen necessities such as pots and pans and dinnerware but not linens and towels.

Most beachfront residences are very close to the water. High tide, in fact, means that the ocean may be almost underneath you. That's not necessarily a good thing, either. With damage from hurricanes and annual winter storms, the matter of continuing beach erosion is a serious issue here (and elsewhere up and down the coast), placing homes perilously close to the water's edge.

There are hundreds of rental homes available all over the island, and they are rented by the week (very few exceptions) by local real estate agents. If you prefer beachfront, ask early. If you don't mind being a few blocks from the beach—and there's good beach access everywhere here—you'll save some money. Speaking of free public access, Edisto has lots of it; just about every block, in fact. (Because of its distance from Charleston and the presence of beaches much closer to that city, like Folly Beach and the Isle of Palms, Edisto doesn't get large numbers of day-trippers.)

Fairfield Ocean Ridge and Bay Creek Villas offer the only real alternative to beach homes. Condos and villas are available in this resort towards the southern end of the beach (turn off Palmetto Boulevard on Lybrand Street to get there). There's a pool at the complex, but to get to the beach you've got to get in your car or take a pretty long stroll, not recommended especially if you're loaded down with beach chairs, cooler, umbrella, and other beach gear. Still, the atmosphere is great, and at Bay Creek the sunsets are terrific.

One note of caution: If you're renting a home on the extreme southern end facing St. Helena Sound, you may find rushing inlet currents that can make swimming prohibitive, even dangerous. Take that into consideration when deciding where to rent at Edisto.

There also is a bed-and-breakfast on the island, something of a rarity along the Palmetto State's coast. Seaside Plantation, a three-story federal home built in 1810, has a wonderfully secluded location just one mile from Edisto Beach.

There's one more lodging option, and it's a dandy. Edisto Beach State Park, right on the ocean, has 96 camping sites, many of them close to the ocean, and five completely furnished and air-conditioned cabins situated on a salt marsh one-and-a-half miles from the beach. They are available on a first-come, first-served basis through the State Park system. Call (843) 869-2156 or (843) 869-2756 or visit the website www.southcarolinaparks.com.

Most sites have water and electrical hookups with restrooms and showers nearby. There are two sites designated for the handicapped. And, while this will come as no news to experienced campers, the bugs can be very aggressive out of doors, especially at sites on the marsh, less so at oceanfront locations where the breeze lessens their annoying impact. Be prepared with repellent.

There are several rental agencies on Edisto Beach that handle just about all of the available homes and condos. Rates for accommodations at tend toward the moderate side, generally lower than Kiawah and Hilton Head rentals, for instance, and a little closer to the rental costs at Pawleys Island. The summer weekly rental for beachfront homes goes from $700 or so to near $4,000 with a good number of units available between $900 and $2,000. Homes within walking range of the beach average $600–$1,800 per week. Condos/villas rent for approximately $200–$375 for a two-night stay in the summer. Off-season rentals will be appreciably lower. A state park cabin rents for $400 a week. There are no super-luxury accommodations for rent at Edisto, and that's one of the things that gives this beach its character.

Dining Out

Edisto has a small but appealing variety of restaurants, the best known of which is the Old Post Office Restaurant on Highway 174 just before you get to the beach. It was a general store at one time and a post office; some of the mailboxes and a window are still around (the post office closed at this location in 1985). The popular restaurant specializes in "Lowcountry Southern cuisine," which may be a tad redundant but which is pretty darned tasty. The emphasis is on fresh local seafood and produce, and it is well prepared. Entrées range up to about $22.

The Pavilion, located at the corner where 174 runs into Palmetto Boulevard, features seafood (surprise!) and is popular for its all-you-can-eat shrimp nights. It's inexpensive and very casual, like everywhere else on the island. Across the street is a service station with some deli food available to eat in or take out. There's also pizza takeout or delivery to anywhere on the island.

On the creek side of the island are several more casual, moderately priced restaurants—Dockside, Jake's, and Sunset Grille—specializing in (guess what?) yummy seafood. You can order other dishes, of course, but if you've come to the coast, why not eat what coastal folks do? It's good, it's fresh. After all, do visitors to Kansas City order shrimp?

Among the other dining options are the Heron House Restaurant in Fairfield and the Gallery Café and Po Pigs BBQ located on the island a few miles from the beach.

Shopping

Please don't come to Edisto because you feel like doing some serious shopping. The few shops here will take care of your basic beach needs, and that's about it. This is really where you come if you want to get away from shopping. There's not a mall here, and there never will be. The basics and a little more are available. So for groceries, beer, beach towels, bug spray, sunscreen, T-shirts, video rentals, a bookstore (with some pretty interesting local histories) and an art gallery, you're fine. Beyond that, crank up the car.

Its small-town pace and out-of-the-way location make Edisto Beach the perfect getaway for nature lovers. (Courtesy South Carolina Department of Parks, Recreation & Tourism)

If you want to rent something during your stay, Island Rentals at the corner of Highway 174 and Palmetto Boulevard has a supply of bikes, strollers, fishing equipment, rafts, kayaks, and even a few boats. You can rent by the hour or the week. Things can get pretty busy in the middle of summer, so consider calling ahead to make a reservation.

Entertainment

The neon and glitz of Myrtle Beach is noticeably absent. There are lots of fun things to do, but just be aware when you arrive that there isn't much of a swingin' night life unless you want to try a little shag dancing on the beach after the sun goes down.

That means the beach—and there's about four miles of it here—is likely to be the focus of your activity, as it should. Edisto has a lovely beach with lots of shells, and it seldom seems crowded. Should you feel trapped by your neighbors, just move down the beach a hundred yards or so and chances are you'll have considerable privacy. Anyone who comes to the beach for the day loves it because of ample free access; every block has a public access path. Just follow the rules and don't litter.

Among the rules: 1) noise ordinance in effect 10 P.M. to 7 A.M., so no loud parties please; 2) no cars on the beach; 3) keep dogs on a leash during the prime beach season; 4) don't touch the sea oats; 5) don't mess with the log-gerhead turtles. Not too tough, eh?

Anything that's connected to the water is fun here: crabbing, fishing (deep-sea or surf), shrimping. You might want to try canoeing or kayaking or even parasailing—with an instructor's guiding hand if you're a novice. And there are fishing trips or river tours offered, too. The Edisto Summer Fest in midsummer celebrates the season with a series of events including shag dance contests, food, races, and lots of music all around the beach.

There's a nature trail for hikers and anyone interested in the island's woodsy marsh environment. It's marked, easy to follow, and a pleasure to stroll unless the bugs are getting to you. It's located just off Highway 174 at the entrance to the state park cabins, about a mile from where the highway reaches Palmetto Boulevard. Bird-watching is a treat, too. There's also an eighteen-hole golf course in the condo development and a driving range, though vacationers whose happiness is found mostly on the links will usually head for other beaches where there are many more options.

Also of interest for visitors will be the opportunities to explore the island's fascinating history. You can hire a knowledgeable and entertaining storyteller for a three- to four-hour car tour of Edisto's plantations, churches, and grave-yards, complete with a ghost story or two (though Edisto lacks the imposing legend of the Gray Man who is said to haunt Pawleys Island a bit farther up the coast). The Edisto Island Preservation Society's Museum—on Highway 174 before you get to the beach—has a number of items, including clothing and baskets and photographs, that document sea island plantation life, the slave history, and the Civil War era. The museum is not open every day of the week, so check when you arrive at the beach for details. There's a small admission fee.

There are several historic churches on Edisto that can be visited, and you can participate in the regularly scheduled worship services. The Presbyterian Church of Edisto Island is the oldest continuous congregation in existence in South Carolina, dating from at least 1710. The current Trinity Episcopal Church building dates from the 1890s, though the church's history goes back as far as the American Revolution. The Old First Baptist Church, from 1818, represents an important part of African American history on the island. There are also Methodist, AME, and Catholic churches on Edisto Island. The Preservation Society is active and presents a number of special programs during the year. Their annual October home and plantation tour is very popular—it's another good reason to visit Edisto away from the summer season.

And finally, if your interest in history goes back a *really* long time ago, you'll be intrigued to know there is some evidence showing that dinosaurs used to roam this area. Of course when that happened it was some 65 million years ago, so don't go looking for Jurassic Park around here. But there have been a number of discoveries of the fossilized remains of long-extinct animals along the coast, and some Edistonians have collected quite a few of them. Their collection is private, but if you call 843-869-3435 when you get to Edisto, the owners are likely to invite you to come over for an informal tour. There's no charge.

FOR MORE INFORMATION call the Edisto Chamber of Commerce, (843) 869-3867, or the Edisto Town Hall, (843) 869-2505. The web site is www.edistochamber.com.

Edisto Beach State Park

The beautiful 1,200-acre park by the sea is understandably among the most popular points in South Carolina's nationally acclaimed state park system. The park has a mile and a half of well-maintained beachfront that is filled with an ever-changing variety of shells. Its natural features include a live oak forest, an expansive salt marsh, and some of the tallest palmetto trees anywhere in South Carolina.

Vacationers who come for the day love Edisto Island State Park. There's a very small admission fee, parking spaces, a great beach to spread out on, a large picnic area, and a gift and souvenir shop. Bring your food and drink, and you're set for the day with about as inexpensive a beach experience as can be arranged. (For information on staying in the park, See Accommodations above.)

Seven

Beaufort and Fripp Island

FOR MORE INFORMATION on Fripp, call (843) 845-4100, visit the website www.FrippIslandResort.com, or write Fripp Island Resort, One Tarpon Boulevard, Fripp Island, SC 29920.

Piracy used to be a bit more respectable enterprise than it is these days. And a good thing, too, else South Carolina's beaches might be named after the likes of Edward Teach, better known as the eighteenth-century pirate Blackbeard. Or maybe John Fripp, though Fripp's piracy at least was officially sanctioned by the British government. Perhaps for that reason Blackbeard lives on in legend while Fripp gave his name to a private island resort where serenity rules over notoriety these days, and $750,000 homes perch over quiet, near-empty beaches. Blackbeard probably wouldn't feel very comfortable at Fripp, but lots of families don't seem to miss his presence when they're enjoying the seclusion and comfort of this upscale island. With two attractive golf courses and a third nearby, a tennis club, a deep-water marina, pools, restaurants, and a beach so uncrowded you could practically lay a football field between the umbrellas, Fripp has a lot going for it. It doesn't have high-rise hotels, a convention center, or quick access to an interstate highway. In other words, Fripp Island is just far enough out of the way to be a perfect vacation point for anyone eager to dodge the frenetic activity that lures hundreds of thousands of visitors to other places along South Carolina's coast each year.

Fripp is part of a triangle of connected beach locations in the lower part of the state. Harbor Island is another private, gated resort that is smaller and a little less high-end. And Hunting Island State Park—located between Harbor Island and Fripp—is arguably the loveliest jewel in South Carolina's park system, with a spectacular beachfront setting. Fripp and Harbor offer no access for day-trippers because they're private, but Hunting Island, which has camping sites as well, is open to everyone for just a small daily fee. Like both Fripp and Harbor, however, it is hardly ever crowded, even in the peak of summer, since all three beaches are at the end of a relatively long stretch of road away from large population areas. Visitors don't just stumble on this trio; they come this way on purpose, and they're usually enchanted by what they find.

Fripp is a barrier island about twenty miles east of Beaufort. Less than half of its 3,000 acres have been developed, and all of that development has come in the last thirty-five or so years. Before that, it was mostly an isolated, lush wilderness, accessible only by boat, where Indians occasionally roamed, where Blackbeard is supposed to have set foot, and where wild boars rooted freely. With the Atlantic Ocean lapping at its front door and tidal marshes curving through the rear, it is a slice of land with a few bluffs barely higher than the water surrounding it, seemingly defying a hurricane-lashed surf to push it back to the mainland.

The inlets and marshes around Fripp made for suitable hiding places for contraband boats during the Civil War. And federal regiments who occupied the South Carolina sea islands beginning in 1862 confiscated all of Fripp as well that same year. After the war's end in 1865, the island was restored to the state after payment of $6.67, a rather paltry sum even then, which could indicate that Fripp was not seen as much of a paradise by its occupiers or anyone else. And in fact, for most of the next century, cut off from the mainland, it remained a dense tropical jungle, home to far more boars, gators, deer, and other wildlife than people.

John Fripp was a planter on nearby St. Helena Island at the end of the seventeenth century who also found time to serve as a British privateer. That enabled him to undertake sometimes risky seafaring voyages to relieve his government's enemies of certain unnecessary goods and riches. Plunder was one word for it. Or, as one of his surprised victims might have bluntly expressed it, "This is nothing short of legalized piracy, sir." Fripp, of course, got to keep a percentage of goods he "rescued," and he apparently used the area around modern-day Fripp Island and uninhabited Pritchards Island to the south as his base of operations.

Fripp is said to have been buried on the island, but the location has long since disappeared. There's also a ghost story heard these days about Fripp's booted footsteps occasionally being found in the sand at the beach, suggesting his return to search for some buried treasure left behind. These days, that treasure most likely would be a found on a golf course.

Development on the island did not begin until 1960. Barges carried bulldozers to begin clearing a path, and in 1964 a bridge to the mainland was constructed that finally opened it to a period of gradual growth of residences and vacation homes. In 1990, a group of investors purchased the island and operated it as the Fripp Company for a decade. It went into new ownership in 2000. Although Fripp is not marketed nationally in the way of the Grand Strand and Hilton Head along the South Carolina coast, it has provided the backdrop for several well-known movies, including the Academy Award–winning *Forrest Gump* and *The Prince of Tides*. The former was filmed in a thick jungle in 1993 that is now part of a golf course—that's how quickly things are changing. The latter film was based on the novel of the same name by Fripp's most famous literary figure, the author Pat Conroy, who has made his home on the island for many years and written rapturously about the sights and smells of the sea island culture ("I am a child of the marsh").

The bridge, privately owned like the island, remains Fripp's only link to the mainland. It has made possible not only the homes and villas and townhouses scattered around Fripp—most blending into the manicured island environment—but golf courses, tennis courts, swimming pools, restaurants, and clubhouses as well. They are a sight that might make old John Fripp's boots turn around and head back out to sea. Or, as a clever entrepreneur, the old fellow these days just might instead be comfortably fixed selling resort property.

Climate

The summer sun can be so hot as to take your breath away. But that's why there's a beach here with an inviting surf, ocean breezes, maybe a shading beach umbrella. And that's why you can be assured of finding plenty of opportunities to work on your tan, too. The summer here is just exactly what you pay for: lots of sun and hot weather. The average high temperature in July is 89. Oh sure, there will be the occasional thundershower, but it's usually of short duration, hardly long enough to require more than a brief detour to the nineteenth hole. Summer is prime time for outdoors activities and for T-shirts and shorts, though some golfers, swimmers, and tennis buffs will prefer to stay inside during the hottest midday hours and focus their energies during the early morning and late afternoon hours. With daylight savings time, there's light enough to play golf until nine P.M. in the middle of summer.

The so-called "shoulder" seasons—spring and fall—have become even more popular with golfers because of the milder weather. And the winter

Palmetto trees line the edge of the Beaufort River along a stretch of the Intracoastal Waterway. (Photograph © 2001 Robert Clark)

months when it is indeed colder seldom turns out to be cold enough to keep most people indoors. The sun shines regularly December through March, the high temperatures average in the low 60s, and sweaters will probably suffice for much of the time. Freezes do occur—there's even been some light snow recorded now and then—but it's not a regular accompaniment to the season. When one of those nor'easters blows over in January or February, however, look for heavy rains, high winds, and a miserable time for a few days, or even a week or so. After that, the sun is back out, the weather is surprisingly mild, and you'll find yourself laughing at those poor folks back home who are digging out of ten inches of snow.

Getting There

Fripp doesn't overflow with visitors because it's a private island, because it doesn't have convention facilities, because it's a comparatively small island, and because it's not easy to get to. Well, it's not really *hard* to get to, it's just that you don't pass it on the way to get to anywhere else. But that's part of its secluded charm, too.

Fripp Island—and Harbor Island and Hunting Island State Park, too—are located at the end of US Highway 21 that runs from Beaufort out to the beaches. And we do mean end. The highway actually dead-ends on Hunting Island and becomes a private road, also paved, that leads to the bridge that carries visitors over to Fripp.

Beaufort—pronounced BUE-fuht, not BOE-fuht, which is the name of the coastal town in North Carolina—is the city closest to Fripp, and the city closest to interstate access. It's a beautiful, small, historic city about twenty-five miles east of Interstate 95, the busy New York-to-Florida route that bisects eastern South Carolina. US 21 links I-95 to Beaufort and then keeps on going through the city heading toward Fripp. Part of the way it's four lanes; between Beaufort and Fripp, it shrinks to two lanes, though construction to widen it is underway. Just stay on 21; you can't get lost.

By the way, Beaufort is well worth a visit; it is a charming, atmosphere-drenched town with a fabulous history, its beautiful antebellum homes seemingly undisturbed by the passage of time and events, and it boasts some unique shops and delightful restaurants. The city's graceful waterfront park affords a relaxing view of traffic on the Intracoastal Waterway. In addition, several movies have been filmed here, including *The Great Santini* (based on the Pat Conroy novel) and the 1980s classic *The Big Chill*. The exterior of the home featured in both films can be seen, although it is privately owned. Inquire for directions at the visitor center, 1006 Bay Street near the water. Call (843) 524-3163. There are lots of lodgings here, partly because the area is being discovered by travelers and partly because of the presence of a couple of important military bases nearby: Parris Island and the Marine Air Station. Parris Island (named for a colonial treasurer of South Carolina) is one of the country's two major "boot camps" for young marines in training. It is open every day to visitors who want a look at marine history and perhaps get a glimpse of the trainees learning how to march and follow orders.

The portion of the road between Beaufort and Fripp can be crowded, depending on the time of day and the time of year, so be patient. There are lots of small roads leading off 21 because there are lots of people who live there, so beware of traffic coming and going. The roadway bridges from Lady's Island to St. Helena Island (the largest of Beaufort County's 65 islands) to Harbor Island to Hunting Island to Fripp Island.

Along the way are some fascinating sights well worth stopping to see. The Penn Center on St. Helena Island has played an important role in African American history from the Civil War up through the civil rights movement a century later. Soon after Union soldiers seized the sea islands in 1862, Quaker missionaries opened the first school for freed slaves at Penn Center. After that, it was an educational, cultural, and community center for the slaves' descendants, and in the 1950s it was where Dr. Martin Luther King Jr. and his colleagues visited regularly while planning their civil rights campaigns. The sixteen buildings and nearly fifty acres that today comprise Penn Center are a National Historic District. There's a museum that records the area's history and documents the Gullah culture of the sea islands. It's open most weekdays, on Land's End Road off Highway 21, approximately halfway between Beaufort and Fripp in the town of Frogmore. Call (843) 838-2011 for details.

One of the region's most intriguing folk art galleries, the Red Piano Too, sits alongside Highway 21 in Frogmore, just about opposite Land's End Road. It's an old wooden grocery, or at least it used to be. Now, listed on the National Register of Historic Places, it houses a remarkable gallery of art works by African American artists, some of them quite well known and priced accordingly, others reflecting the imagination of self-taught artists. It's a great break on your trip from Beaufort to Fripp.

And while you're driving, other sights are eye-catching, too. There are myriad creeks, marshes, and even the Intracoastal Waterway that wind through this area, so the views can be magnificent. Shrimp boats are visible on both sides of the road, and once you get to Hunting Island, the lush greenery crowds close to the road. The Spanish moss hangs low, evoking a closed-in, heavy atmosphere and a long-ago time when horses pulled carriages down narrow dirt roads to the dock for occupants to board a tiny boat to the island. At night, this little drive can be darkly mysterious. Slow down. Savor it.

A delightful and unusual side trip awaits those who have the time to take a left turn off US 21 on state highway 802 heading toward Coosaw Island. That's the jumping-off place for one of the guided boat tours of the ACE Basin, one of the largest undeveloped marine estuaries on the East Coast. That area of salt marshes, tidal creeks, and old rice fields is where the salt and fresh waters of the Ashepoo, Combahee, and Edisto Rivers (old Indian names whose initials form the basin's name, A-C-E) join to create a remarkable wetlands wilderness. The tours include views of waterfowl and eagles and the habitats of dozens of creatures. Plan on 3 to 4 hours for your tour. There are other departure points for ACE Basin tours in Charleston and Edisto Beach.

There is not an airport on Fripp, but the Beaufort County Airport can accommodate private planes, and it is just off Highway 21 near Beaufort, about sixteen miles from Fripp. There is no rental car office at the airstrip, but you can take a cab into Beaufort to pick up a rental. If you arrive by boat, there is a marina on the island.

Getting Oriented

Figuring out Fripp doesn't require rocket science. The 3,000-acre island is separated from undeveloped Pritchards Island at its sound end by Skull Inlet (named, of course, after travelers who had some unlucky encounters with pirates a few centuries back). It boasts more than three miles of beach along the Atlantic.

After driving over the bridge from the mainland, you'll come to a security gate barring all but residents, guests, and others with a designated purpose for being on the island. To your right is the driveway to the Fripp resort offices, where you will pick up the keys to your rental unit, reserve a golf cart complete with roof and windshield, and get a map. After driving past the security guards, you'll be on Tarpon Boulevard, which parallels and runs close to the oceanfront, passing the Beach Club about halfway to the end of the island. Tarpon dead-ends at the south end in front of Skull Inlet. Just past the Beach Club, Bonito Road turns off to the right and dead-ends at the marina. The road to Ocean Creek Golf Course turns left off Bonito and will take visitors to the middle part of the south end of the island. To reach developments on the island's north end, turn left on Remora Drive, about a mile from the security gate, which winds its way to Ocean Point Golf Course and homes and villas. A left turn on Fiddler's Trace off Tarpon about a half mile from the security gate leads to houses and villas on the marsh.

The Beach Club is the location for restaurants, the tennis center, shops, pools, and villas. There's a restaurant and rental shop at the marina, and the Cabana Club and Veranda Beach at the south end past Ocean Creek course has a snack bar, a boutique, and more pools. There's another restaurant at the north end where Ocean Point course begins.

These locations are all within a short driving distance of one another. But the favored mode of transportation on Fripp is the easily rented electric golf cart. They are as ubiquitous as the sand flea and the easiest and most economical way to get around. You'll find parking areas for them all over the island. If you're driving a car, be careful; the carts don't move quickly and often have lots of youngsters on board. There are paved bike paths, and the walking is fun, too. Everything moves at a little slower pace here, and you'll enjoy it more if you slow down and adjust to it.

Accommodations

You can rent a private home, a villa, a bungalow, or a cottage, and you can be close to whatever fuels your dreams: the ocean, the golf course, the tennis courts, or the marsh. Rates are highest in the summer months, approximately mid-May to the first of September, and lowest in the winter, December through February. During the summer months, rentals are weekly-only for all vacation homes and many oceanfront and ocean view villas. All are well furnished. Rentals run Saturday to Saturday in some cases, Sunday to Sunday in others. For the best selection, reservations should be made early in the year; some popular oceanfront and golf locations are reserved a year in advance, so it's hard to be accused of being too early here. There are more than three

Fripp Island is a paradise for those looking for golfing, tennis, sailing—or just relaxing on the beaches of its private resort community. (Courtesy Fripp Island Resort)

hundred units available for rentals on the island, but oceanfront locations are limited, of course, and they are the most expensive. A few of them are pretty luxurious, too, so if you want some high-style living for a week or two, Fripp should do very nicely.

There are more than a hundred private homes available for rental, and they range from oceanfront mansions to rustic beach bungalows. The largest can accommodate up to eighteen people. Summer rates vary from $1,200 to about $3,800, with many homes in the $1,800–$2,300 range. The rates fall by about one-third in the spring and fall and close to half in some cases during the winter months.

Villas are located around the island and are priced for that. Oceanfront and ocean views get the highest rates, a two-bedroom unit averaging between $1,000 and $1,600 a week in the summer. The older Captain John Fripp Villas are closest to the Beach Club and are a little more crowded than the others; of course, you're also closer to the many Beach Club facilities, too, as well as being within a few steps of the beach.

Tree House units are pedestal houses in the marshes and are very private, though they require either long walks or a golf cart to get to the beach. Other units snuggle up to pools or fairways or tennis courts. There are cottages with ocean or inlet views and several bungalows at Veranda Beach on the south end. A two-bedroom bungalow goes for around $275 a night in the summer, with a 15 percent discount offered for stays of seven nights or more.

Not all the homes and villas on Fripp are for rental. There is a small community of year-round residents here, with an active property-owners association and special activities in out-of-summer months when many visitors have gone back home.

There are less expensive villa and condo units for rent on nearby Harbor Island (see that section, following, for information). And Hunting Island State Park has two hundred inexpensive camping sites and fifteen cabins for rent throughout the year (details on those in the section following).

Dining Out

The island isn't exactly awash with dining options, but there are more than might be expected given Fripp's relatively small size and the fact that this is a private resort island. Dress is casual; shirts and shoes are required at all but the outdoor snack bars. The restaurant at the Beach Club is open for dinner and has seating upstairs and downstairs and outdoor buffets in nice weather. The menu features entrées up to about $25, with fresh seafood usually available. The tables look out on a pool area or the ocean, and there's a Sunday brunch buffet. The recently renovated Bonito Boathouse at the marina has two levels of seating, including an upstairs glassed-in porch with beautiful sunset views over the marsh. Fried shrimp, scallops, and fish are among the culinary pleasures here.

Sandals at the Cabana Club on the south end offers lunches and light suppers during the summer, while Hugo's on the north end has breakfast, lunch, and dinner. Take-out pizza is featured here, too. The Nineteenth Hole at Ocean Creek also serves up breakfast and lunch.

If you don't mind driving a few miles off Fripp, you'll find one of the best-kept secrets of the lowcountry (except to locals and visitors who keep coming back time after time). It's called the Shrimp Shack, a very casual, weather-beaten wooden shack with a screened-in porch where a hungry folks congregate for some fine shrimpburgers (no kidding!)—fresh shrimp meat fried up into a sizzling hot, scrumptious patty. You can practically watch the fresh shrimp being unloaded daily, and it's only a matter of minutes before the catch is ready for eating. A shrimpburger plate including French fries and slaw is about $6. You can eat either in the screened-in porch or outside, where the bugs will sometimes battle you for the goodies. In Frogmore, the Gullah House restaurant offers more local specialties, and Beaufort a few miles farther away has a variety of restaurants, local and fast-food, in all price ranges.

Entertainment

Fripp, not surprisingly, doesn't draw much of a late-night crowd. After all, most people are here for the beach or some golf or tennis or just relaxing, so their focus is on daylight activities. There are plenty of them.

The beach at Fripp is delightful. Because erosion affects different parts of the beach differently, the beaches can take on looks that vary from year to year. Over much of the north end, the beaches are wide at high tide and very wide at low tide. The joke has been recently that visitors needed a golf cart to get from their oceanfront house to the surf. High tide at other parts of the island can send the surf crashing up closer to the homes. Regardless, Fripp enjoys attractive, clean beaches, and there's good shelling, too. The surf is pretty calm most of the time. There are marked paths at regular intervals providing access to the beach at various points along the oceanfront. Of course there are no day visitors here, so the beaches are occupied only by resort guests and residents. The access points also allow for the parking of golf carts by the side of the road.

Golf is very popular. There are two excellent eighteen-hole courses on the island and a third a short distance away. The new Ocean Creek course is the first signature course designed by PGA champion Davis Love III. Its 6,629 yards play out over salt marshes and wetlands negotiated through a network of wooden walkways and bridges. It's a testing, classic par 71 that won top-ten honors in new course design from *Golf* magazine and *The Golfer.* There's a pro shop, and lessons are offered.

Ocean Point Court is a par 72, 6,556-yard layout designed by George W. Cobb that has some nice ocean vistas and inlet views. The pro shop is fully stocked, and golfers of all abilities can check out the clinics here. The two courses are no more than ten minutes by cart from anywhere on the island. A third layout, South Carolina National Golf Club, another Cobb design, is an eighteen-hole course on Cat Island, about twenty miles from Fripp; there are pro shop, restaurant, and lounge there. There's a central reservations number for tee times at all three courses (800-933-0050). The resort has specially priced golf packages, including several for foursomes. Groups up to three hundred people per course are welcomed (although somebody is likely to have to tee it up before 7 A.M.).

The Fripp Racquet Club has ten year-round courts on the middle of the island opposite the Beach Club. During the summer, there are all kinds of instructional opportunities, including tournaments and clinics. There are programs for youngsters from four to sixteen in season. If you've got some special requests for your visit, contact the pro shop before your arrival. Resort guests get one free hour of court time per unit per day during their stay.

An array of seashells adorns a Beaufort-area beach in early spring.
(Photograph © 2001 Robert Clark)

If you're into swimming but don't care for the surf, there are several pools around the island. The largest is at the Cabana Club on the south end. Actually, there are three pools here: an oval heated for spring and fall (though beware—the heating is minimal for some tastes), a lagoon pool with a misty cave and flower-edged waterfalls, and a kiddie pool. There are a couple of pools at the Beach Club in the middle of the island, one specially for families, the other just for grownups. And there's another pool at the north end. All pools are free for the use of guests at the resort, and it's easy to sign up for lessons.

Walking, biking, and golf-carting are the easiest ways to get around and provide their own entertainment, and there are miles of scenic paths where you're more likely to run into a deer than an automobile. But you also can rent a boat or kayak for scooting around the waterways, and deep-sea fishing charters can be arranged.

Speaking of fishing, there are several ways to try and hook the big one around the island. Half-day or full-day charters will take you out to sea, or you can try your luck casting in the surf. And at the entrance to the Fripp Bridge on Hunting Island is Paradise Pier, a fishing pier that juts out nearly 1,200 feet into the waters of Fripp Inlet. There's a small fee for admission to the pier; you can rent equipment there. Because it is not a part of the resort, anyone, whether a guest or not, is welcome to use the pier facilities.

"Camp Fripp" has lots of activities for kids during the summer months and holidays. Youngsters between the ages of four and twelve have special partial-day programs, and there are adventures designed for family groups, including canoe trips, crabbing, and naturalist walks. Teens will enjoy volleyball, canoeing, casino nights, dances, and basketball.

And just in case you don't get enough exercise swimming or walking, there's a fitness center at the Beach Club with Cybex equipment, stationary bikes, and other aerobic exercise equipment.

Shopping

Shopping is a minimalist adventure here. There are no large stores, outlets, or malls within sight. You'll have to drive to Beaufort for that. Fripp does have several small retail shops offering pretty much what you would expect: beachwear, casual clothing, and island-logo items from umbrellas to hats. The golf pro shop has golf equipment and apparel, and the tennis center stocks tennis-related items. The Rhett Gallery at the Beach Club might be a little unexpected, however; it sells lowcountry prints and paintings, something a little different as a souvenir. The marina sells boat supplies and also gas for boats and cars, along with some party supplies like beer.

At the Visitor Center, where guests check in when they arrive, there are a couple of small boutiques and the T. T. Bones General Store, something of an island icon. Lots of residents (and visitors, too) do a little shopping here when they're running short of bread or milk or potato chips. The store also has an area where liquor may be purchased as well as beer, and you can rent videos. By the way, be sure to leave a little change for the cats who hang around. They're not beggars, but the money goes to keep them in cat food. The closest larger grocery to Fripp is at Frogmore, with lots of additional choices a few miles farther away in Beaufort.

If you like art, by the way, don't fail to stop at the Red Piano Too Gallery on St. Helena Island between Beaufort and Fripp. The gallery specializes in work by artists of the region, many of them African Americans, and their work reflects Southern and Gullah influences.

Harbor Island Resort

FOR INFORMATION about Harbor Island Resort, call (800) 809-2410 or (843) 838-2410 or go to www.HarborIslandSC.com.

....

Driving from Beaufort on Highway 21, you'll reach 1,700-acre Harbor Island before you get to Fripp. It's fifteen miles from Beaufort (about four miles from its larger sister resort) and considerably more compact than Fripp. Only recently developed, it's a gated resort with homes and multi-rise villa units for rent throughout the year. It doesn't have quite all of the charm and lushness of Fripp, perhaps, but its rental rates are less expensive, generally between $800 and $2,000 for a one-week stay in the summer months. Limited daily rentals are available. A multipurpose meeting center can accommodate small groups. The resort has two-and-a-half miles of unspoiled, uncrowded beach, much of it fronting the waters of St. Helena Sound. Don't look for big ocean waves here.

The Harbor Island Beach & Racquet Club has four fast-dry tennis courts, a pro shop, Olympic and kiddie swimming pools, a children's playground area, a volleyball court, a fitness center, and a casual café and lounge. Guests are entitled to one free hour of tennis court time per rental. In addition, guests at Harbor Island can enjoy free access to everything at Fripp, including golf, tennis, and restaurants. Free sightseeing to Paradise Pier on Hunting Island is another treat for guests. Bike rentals are available, but because of its distance from Fripp's amenities, a car is a necessity for getting around here.

Hunting Island State Park

FOR INFORMATION about Hunting Island, call (843) 838-2011 or go to www.southcarolinaparks.com.

The large island—sixteen miles from Beaufort on US 21 and just before you get to Fripp—has been unobtrusively converted from its natural environment into a state park in recent years, and it is surely among the loveliest of parks anywhere in the nation. With some five thousand acres of semitropical beauty and an abundance of wildlife, not to mention nearly four miles of incredibly gorgeous beachfront, it will take your breath away. The wide beach divides the ocean from sand dunes, a maritime forest, and salt marshes. Picturesque bone-like driftwood sculptures left by cypress and pine trunks are scattered nearby. Standing on the white sand beach, it's hard to know in which direction the scenery is more spectacular. Parts of the beach are for use by swimmers; others are open to surf fishers. There are comfort stations and picnic areas clearly marked, and a ranger interpretive center that is open year-round.

Hunting Island has one of the few remaining lighthouses on the Atlantic coast, built in 1875. At 140 feet above the ground, it gives visitors who climb the steps to the top a great 180-degree view of the coast. It is no longer in operation, and it has been re-located twice to shield it from the advancing ocean. Like the park, it is open year-round.

Built in 1875, the lighthouse at Hunting Island is one of the few remaining lighthouses on the Atlantic coast. (Photograph © 2001 Robert Clark)

There are two hundred campsites for rent, with a limited number available by reservation. The rest are rented on a first-come, first-served basis, so get there early if you want to stake your claim in summer (call 843-838-2011). Each site has electrical hookups and is close to showers and restrooms. There are also a few cabins that come completely furnished and are heated and air-conditioned (not to be sneezed at in the middle of July). There's an on-site camp store for supplying visitors with basic needs.

Hunting was once part of a chain of islands—including Pritchards Island, Fripp Island, and Harbor Island—that acquired the name "Hunting" from the richness of wildlife. During most of its existence, in fact, Hunting Island was without a resident population, serving instead as a hunters' paradise, first for the native Indians, then later for wealthy visitors from the North.

There's a small daily admission fee to get into Hunting Island that covers parking your car. It seems a bargain given the haunting beauty of this state park, understandably one of the most popular in the South Carolina system. It's open 6 A.M. to 9 P.M. April through September and 6 A.M. to 6 P.M. October to March.

Eight

Hilton Head Island

FOR INFORMATION call the Hilton Head Chamber of Commerce, (843) 785-3673, or (800) 523-3373 or visit the website, www.hiltonheadisland.org.

A playground for the wealthy. A resort development internationally acclaimed for its environmental sensitivity. Home to richly endowed antebellum sea island cotton plantations. And the first place in the South where slaves were freed during the Civil War. Hilton Head has both enjoyed and suffered an amazing history.

It has been transformed in the space of less than a half century from an isolated, thinly populated barrier island to one of the largest, best-known, and most successful resort locales along the Atlantic coast. Travel sections in the largest newspapers across the country carry the advertising of Hilton Head. Nationally circulated magazines tout its charms. The world's best golfers arrive each spring after the Masters to play in the newly named WorldCom Classic–Heritage of Golf tournament. Many of the global tennis stars of the last two decades have lobbed and volleyed here at the Family Circle Tennis Classic. Former president Bill Clinton and his family and many of America's top thinkers spent many New Year's vacations at the island's "Renaissance Weekend." In choosing its most influential figures of the twentieth century, one South Carolina newspaper selected Hilton Head Island because of its international prominence and the enormous focus of attention it has drawn to the Palmetto State.

Many headline-makers, CEOs, and military officers have decided to make the island their retirement home; the average income of Hilton Head residents is higher than you'll find anywhere else in South Carolina. Most of its residents are not natives. The story goes that when strangers are approached in Charleston, the first question asked is, "Where are you from?" In Hilton Head, the question will be, "Where in Ohio are you from?" It's just a story, but the island has long been a popular refuge for Midwesterners.

With its exquisite resort status have come problems that beset many communities: traffic congestion, quality-of-life issues in environment and construction, and concerns about the income gap between the island's wealthiest homeowners, mostly white, and workers, mostly black, who service the booming tourist industry and who cannot afford to live on the island. Hilton Head is a bit of everything—and anything—you'd like it to be. If you want to confront social issues here, they await. If you wish to savor the luxury and style and class of Hilton Head, the invitation is out. It is a great place to have a great time. And while there are ways to enjoy the island's pleasures without spending big chunks of money, the fact is that most of the vacationers who come to Hilton Head do so in expectation of spending more than a little money for the trip.

Looking at Hilton Head Island from the ocean side gives the appearance of a foot with the toes pointed to the south past Savannah. It is the southernmost barrier island on the South Carolina coast, and with forty-two square miles it's the largest. It is twelve miles long and five miles wide. The beachfront is long and lovely and justly famous. It is also not exactly secluded; development here has been extensive. If you're staying at a large luxury resort hotel, you won't be alone when you wander out to the beach. Chances are you won't be alone either when you drive out to a restaurant or a movie or one of the many golf courses or tennis courts. Hilton Head is not a secret in travel circles. That doesn't mean you won't find wonderful moments of quiet togetherness on the island; they abound. But the same person who champions the "Arrogantly Shabby" of Pawleys Island, for instance, or the loose play-it-like-it-is attitude of Folly Beach, will not be eager to head for upscale Hilton Head. It's all about choices, and one of the greatest delights about the beaches in South Carolina is that they are very different, affording beachgoers an abundance, even a richness, of choices.

Until 1956 when a bridge was built to the mainland, Hilton Head was accessible only by boat. Back then, there existed few roads—none paved—no electricity, no water system, no golf courses, no resort hotels. The island's history had disappeared as surely as the old cotton plantations that once furnished great wealth for sea island planters.

Hilton Head combines a laid-back island lifestyle with beautifully designed surroundings, for vacationers and full-time residents alike. (Courtesy Hilton Head Island Chamber of Commerce)

And then came Charles Fraser, who is appropriately credited with the development of Hilton Head, creating an environmentally friendly resort community that became a model for dozens of latter-day locations all over the world.

Fraser's idea was to build a golf and retirement resort that would appeal to the wealthy, offering seclusion, privacy, and luxury. Echoing the island's history, he chose to name his resort community Sea Pines Plantation, and he acquired a little over five thousand acres—about the size of Hunting Island slightly to the north of Hilton Head—at the island's southern end. Unfortunately, the only good location for a bridge and road linking the island to the mainland was towards the north end, a winding distance of close to twenty-five miles. That considerably escalated the costs for developing the island, but interestingly, it helped assure a focused growth for Hilton Head's early years.

Fraser's plan for constructing Sea Pines called for connecting human occupants with the natural environment. In other words, he didn't want to bulldoze acres of grand live oaks and palmettos and clear out underbrush to build freestanding, architecturally unprepossessing homes. Instead, he hired architects to put up homes of subdued design that blended in size and color with the landscape. Beachfront homes were built far back from the ocean to protect sand dunes. Lagoons dug for fresh water served as scenic views for homes nearer the forests that covered the island. Fraser's vision proved popular. More and more people arrived, and other developers chose to follow his design style. Fraser created Harbour Town within Sea Pines, a small community of shops and homes built around a red-and-white lighthouse. Tennis, restaurants, condominiums, an inn, and other trappings of growth soon followed. National attention was always close by; in the late 1960s the Southern Governors held their annual meeting here.

Other developers began work on sites on the north end of the island, also adopting methods pioneered by Fraser with their own resort "plantations," most with beach frontage. What was initially a lonely and lovely drive from the bridge to Sea Pines Plantation began drawing thousands of motorists daily, who passed through developing tracts of land. That same drive, Highway 278, or the William Hilton Parkway, bisects Hilton Head now, looking nothing like it did in the 1950s and '60s. With plantation development successful, major hotel chains like Hyatt, Hilton, and Marriott followed, putting up large, highrise but discreetly placed beachfront units. The Disney Corporation arrived in the 1990s, too. From the bridge to Sea Pines, homes and villas popped up accompanied by stores, restaurants, malls, and shopping centers for the growing numbers of retirees, residents, and vacationers. Hilton Head now has a resident population of over 30,000 and draws more than two million visitors each year to its dozens of hotels, golf courses, and tennis courts, staggering numbers surely unimagined by Fraser and his earliest successors.

What will visitors today find on Hilton Head?

Hilton Head is a bustling, upscale, spread-out island—don't go looking for downtown because there is no "downtown" area as such. It has some very pricey real estate—seven figures and up and up—some of the nicest hotels and villas on the coast, a multitude of stores and restaurants, a perhaps surprising but enterprising arts and cultural scene, enough world-class golf courses and tennis courts and activities to fill an entire summer, much less a week or two, and a diversity of vacation costs from the sort-of-moderate to the very expensive.

And like many a well-heeled dowager, it comes with quite a past, too.

For hundreds of years, Indian tribes roamed the island and nearby mainland, hunting and fishing from its rich, undisturbed land. The Spanish made two landings in the early sixteenth century but established no settlements. The island acquired its name from Captain William Hilton, who arrived from Barbados and claimed it for England in 1663. Either Hilton wasn't a good salesman, or his English employers couldn't foresee golf courses, for it was seven years later before the English got around to their permanent settlement in the new colony of Carolina at the site of present-day Charleston. Over the next century, however, planters found success growing cotton in the fertile soil and became among the most prosperous of all Americans, thanks in no small part to the labor of a growing number of slaves. Interestingly, one of the most prosperous plantations then is today the site of a golf course in Sea Pines.

When the Civil War began in 1861, Confederates threw up earthen forts to protect their important cotton-producing plantations, one on the northern end of the island and another across Port Royal Sound from the first one, on St. Phillips Island (uninhabited today). They lasted not much longer than it took to construct them. The Federal navy sailed into Port Royal Sound in November 1861, demolished the barricades, chased away the Confederate defenders, and landed an amphibious force of nearly 13,000 soldiers, a miraculous and challenging feat not rivaled in size until World War II.

The occupation of Hilton Head lasted for the duration of the war and saw the creation of a most unusual community to serve the troops: bookstores, restaurants, hotels, tattoo parlors, liquor stores, "sort of like it turned out a century later," one slightly cynical historian has observed. The Union troops moved easily into nearby Beaufort and the neighboring sea islands, seizing the property now abandoned by plantation owners and releasing their slaves (many of whom had been left behind by their hastily fleeing owners). Some of those slaves eventually entered the U.S. army; others began farming the small parcels of land carved out of the old plantations. A school for the freedmen was begun at the Penn Center near Beaufort. When the war ended, planters returned seeking their land, much of it devastated. Some deeds now belonging to former slaves were invalidated, but other slaves retained their land. The island's once-rich economy, however, had been shattered.

By the end of the nineteenth century, cotton was again being produced on Hilton Head, but on a scale much smaller than before the war. And production dropped even more with the destruction and virtual elimination of the crop caused by the boll weevil beginning in the 1920s. Subsistence farming, oystering, shrimping, and crabbing provided a way of life for the island's residents into the Depression—along with the production of illegal whiskey (the island's isolation made illegal whiskey stills difficult to reach for federal agents). Wealthy northerners purchased large parcels of land for use as hunting preserves, and forestry operations provided modest income for others. Thus Hilton Head languished in quietude until the arrival of Charles Fraser, an island virtually as isolated as two hundred years before. Entering a new and uncharted century, Hilton Head now is an institution where, as one clever writer has expressed it, "the spirit of the Home Shopping Network struggles with the soul of *Architectural Digest.*"

When to Go

Short answer: Whenever you can, as soon as you can. The weather will almost certainly be hot in the summer, warm in the spring and fall and mild in the winter months. What else do you need? In the summer, the temperatures will climb into the 90s, maybe even the low 100s for a few days. It will be humid, and you will praise the invention of air conditioning. Mosquitoes and the tiny no-see-ums (that's why they got the name) can bug you, too. But that's a typical South Carolina lowcountry June, July, August, and early September.

Every imaginable outdoor activity is running full-tilt during that period. In the "shoulder" seasons of spring and fall—basically March to mid-May and mid-September into December—Hilton Head is even more of a golfer's paradise than it is the rest of the year. The high temperatures glide into the 70s, the sun shines, there's an ocean breeze . . . and a golf course looks like Mecca. Tennis fans are no less enthusiastic. And the winter months, December through February, are hardly worse. You can certainly expect some cold days, so if you're visiting in January, bring your sweaters. But along the coast, even in the most bitter of months, warm days follow cold ones, and it's never cold for long. And there are some very good things about the winter season, too, like lower rates and fewer crowds (though Hilton Head is now busy year-round). This is a great time to get on the courts or the links, though the ocean water will be too chilly for all but the bravest. Don't be surprised by the sight of Canadians in T-shirts and shorts, no matter the chilly air.

Precipitation isn't a vacation-spoiler at Hilton Head. You're just about more likely to spot a sled dog than you are to experience snowfall on the island. It does rain, of course, but afternoon summer thunderstorms seldom hang around long, and there are so many things to do at Hilton Head no matter the weather that you shouldn't be overly concerned. Bottom line: hot in summer, nice most of the rest of the time. If you're coming here from a cold climate, you can't help but be delighted by what you'll find regardless of when you arrive.

Getting There

Hilton Head Island is about thirty miles north of Savannah—it can take forty-five minutes to an hour to get there, however—and some ninety miles south of Charleston. There are plenty of signs along Interstate 95 directing drivers to the island, and once you get on four-lane Highway 278, it leads directly to the island. The first bridge to Hilton Head was a two-lane toll bridge in 1956. These days, an ever-growing stream of vehicles cross over a four-lane, toll-free bridge and pour onto the island. In the mornings and afternoons, traffic routinely backs up with visitors, residents, and workers heading to or returning from work on the island.

Most people arrive by car. But there are six marinas where you can dock your boat: Harbour Town Yacht Basin and South Beach Marina, both in Sea Pines; Palmetto Bay Marina on Calibogue Sound; Shelter Cove Marina in Palmetto Dunes, Skull Creek Marina in Skull Creek; and Windmill Harbour Marina in Windmill Harbour.

If you're flying into Hilton Head, there's a small but well-equipped airport on the north end of the island where private planes are easily accommodated (and some very nice private planes use this airport, too). USAirways Express provides limited daily passenger service to Charlotte, North Carolina. The closest major airport is at Savannah, about forty-five miles away, and nonstop flights are available from there on nine airlines to a number of major cities. There are shuttles available at the airport to take passengers to the island, or you can rent a car.

Getting Oriented

Hilton Head Island's foot-shaped landscape is pointed toward the south. Sea Pines, the original development on the island, is at the south end, and so is Harbour Town, whose red-and-white-striped lighthouse is the most enduring symbol of Hilton Head Island. Port Royal Sound enters the Atlantic on the north end, and the waters of Calibogue Sound flow around the back of the island past the south end.

Besides Sea Pines, the other resort plantations are found in the middle and northern end of Hilton Head. Hilton Head Plantation is the northernmost resort area, with property facing on Skull Creek on the back side of the island and Port Royal Sound. Palmetto Hall (no beachfront access) is adjacent, while Port Royal Plantation, with beachfront locations, is situated next to it. Continuing south, Palmetto Dunes is the next resort, with Shipyard bumping up against it, and then Sea Pines. Inland developments include Indigo Run, Yacht Cove, Shelter Cove, Wexford, and Long Cove Club. Two other areas, Windmill Harbour and Spanish Wells, have access to Calibogue Sound on the back side of the island.

The four-lane William Hilton Parkway bisects much of the island, stretching for twenty-five miles from the bridge connecting Hilton Head to the mainland, making a long curve southward in the direction of the island's toes, then heading down to about the middle of the island. From there into Sea Pines at the southern end, follow Greenwood Drive, or, along the ocean side, on Sea Pines Drive. The Parkway dead-ends at Sea Pines Circle, a busy, circular confluence of businesses at the entrance to Sea Pines.

The Parkway is four lanes and passes most of the resort communities and businesses on the island. There are lots of traffic lights along the way and lots of traffic, and it can be very crowded and make for slow going, especially in the morning and afternoon. There is, however, an excellent new alternative. The Cross Island Expressway, a limited access, multilane toll road ($1) bypass, avoids some of the heaviest traffic on the Parkway, diverting vehicles heading toward the southern end of the island and dodging the traffic lights and backups that beset the Parkway. If your destination is the south end, the bypass will speed you close to the entrance to the Sea Pines Circle. If, however, your destination is one of the other resorts or oceanfront hotels or the malls or other businesses, the Parkway likely is the better way, even with its occasional delays.

There's good signage on the island, but sometimes your destination can sneak up on you because most businesses have been designed in environmentally appropriate ways. Fast-food outlets don't always look quite like they do in the midst of big cities. And the entrances to some of the resorts can surprise the unwary. Be alert and look for the signs. There are several public beach access points at the north and the middle, too. Wherever you go and whenever, don't expect to get lonely. Hilton Head stays busy at all times of the year, whether it's prime-time summer activity, golfing off-season, or just year-round residents doing their grocery shopping.

Since the island is so busy and spread out, a car is almost a necessity unless you're planning to spend all of your time in one place. The key word here is "almost," because there are miles of public bike paths that make biking always a friendly choice. Electric carts are used in the resorts and plantations but never on major roadways. Carts and bikes are easily rented. Walking is fun, too, at least along the beach. Once you get around the Parkway, however, the steady flow of traffic will discourage all but the foolhardy. Taxis provide service night and day as well.

Accommodations

There are more than 3,000 hotel and motel rooms, and nearly 6,000 rooms in villas, condos and townhouses, and timeshares on the island. What's amazing is that there's still as much undeveloped land on the island as there is. Hilton Head easily can handle everything from a family group packed into a minivan to busloads of conventioneers. On a busy weekend, the island can play host to perhaps 50,000 people. And those guests can choose among a variety of locations, from beachfront to inlet views, from forested landscapes to lagoon homes. The price ranges go from the very moderate to the very high. Because there are so many places to stay here, it's critical to figure out what you're look-ing for before you make reservations. And by the way, you can almost always find accommodations at Hilton Head at the last minute, though the choice rooms are likely to be taken.

The major beachfront resort hotels can be reached off the Parkway. The Westin Resort has the northernmost location on the island. Moving south-ward you will pass such familiar names as Hyatt, Hilton, Crowne Plaza, Holi-day Inn, and Marriott at the southern end (though it is not at the southern end of the island, which is part of the private Sea Pines resort). All of the hotels are highly ranked by national rating services, and all have a high level of service, including their own pools just in case you don't feel like a little surf action. The summer rates range from $225 upward to around $375 a night for a two-bedroom unit; off-season rates drop by nearly half.

There are other hotels and motels that do not have oceanfront locations and are accordingly lower-priced. For those looking to enjoy Hilton Head at its least expensive, these can be bargains when used with the free public beach within relatively short driving distance. They include such chains as Hampton Inn, Shoney's Inn, Red Roof, Motel 6, Fairfield Inn, Residence Inn, and Com-fort Inn. Most have pools, and a few have restaurants on the premises. The summer rates are quite reasonable, with a range of about $60 (if you're lucky) to $175 per night, and in the off-season, they drop even lower.

Sea Pines is the best-known of the traditional plantations and the largest in size. If you desire beachfront locations, you'll want to investigate Sea Pines, Shipyard, Palmetto Dunes, and Port Royal; the others are not on the ocean. There are numerous housing options in the plantation communities, and the rates go higher with the proximity to the beach and the luxury of the accom-modations. Nightly rentals in summer for a two-bedroom unit range from around $150 to $275, depending on location. Similar rates apply for other resorts around the island. Weekly rentals start at about $800 and go up over $2,000.

Access to golf courses is important for many visitors, and there's hardly any place on Hilton Head that isn't close to one. If you want to stay next to the fairway, that's easily arranged, too. Those accommodations will likely cost between $125 and $300 per night for a two-bedroom unit in summer.

Disney is here as well. The company's Hilton Head Resort has cottages and resort villas at its location in Shelter Cove (which is not on the ocean), with summer rentals going for up to $300 for a two-bedroom unit.

Nearly all establishments on the island offer special packages with reduced rates at various times of the year—some even in the summer months. Golf and tennis packages are very popular, and there are others designed specially for large groups. Hilton Head has excellent convention facilities for thousands of people. Contact the specific resort or the Chamber of Commerce if you want to know more about conventions or large group assemblies (800-523-3373 or www.hiltonheadisland.org)

For general advice about accommodations on the island, call the Hilton Head Central Reservations number, (800) 785-7018 or (843) 785-9050, or www.hiltonheadcentral.com.

Dining

You can enjoy a meal on land or water. You can pay a lot or a little. You can find as nearly as many cuisines represented on the island as you can in a large American city. And you can go nuts trying to eat in all of the restaurants to be found on Hilton Head—almost as nuts as you'll be trying to get in one of the nice ones on Saturday night without a reservation. Seafood is the main ingredient on menus, but your options include Southern barbecue, wood-fired brick pizza, German entrées, Italian, Irish, Mexican, Chinese, French, Indian, Japanese . . . well, let your imagination be your guide.

As with the range in prices for accommodations—from luxurious surroundings and oceanfront views to unpretentious motels tucked away from the beach—so do dining costs vary wildly. If you're on a tight budget, there are plenty of fast-food outlets and small, inexpensive restaurants catering to your less-expensive needs. Most of them are located adjacent to the William Hilton Parkway as it winds its way through the island. The Hilton Head Diner in the middle of the island is very popular and not expensive; it serves up burgers and fries and also has a full bar. The Salty Dog Café on South Beach in Sea Pines also is a must for many visitors who seem to relish its famous T-shirts as much as the inexpensive food.

Higher-end restaurants and lounges line the Parkway, too and they also may be found in the resort areas and hotels. For instance, the Barony Grill at the Westin Resort is one of the most highly praised restaurants on the island,

and so is Hemingway's at the Hyatt Regency. Reservations are a necessity, especially during the summer season and on weekends, at those and other fine dining establishments such as the Nantucket Seafood House near Sea Pines Circle, Harbourmaster's in Shelter Cove, Starfire Contemporary Bistro in Orleans Plaza, and Two Eleven Park Wine & Bistro near Sea Pines Circle. Casual attire is acceptable in the evenings.

And if you'd prefer to eat on the water, there are sunset dinner charters that serve up meals while you savor the views offshore. In brief, there's no reason to be hungry or thirsty anywhere during your visit to Hilton Head—or the waters around it.

Golf

There are thirty-two public and private golf courses on or close to Hilton Head Island, all but two of them challenging eighteen-hole layouts. Some of the world's best players, from Jack Nicklaus and Arnold Palmer to Tiger Woods and Davis Love III (who has won the island's prestigious PGA event, the WorldCom tournament, an amazing four times) have toured the courses before cheering crowds. Visitors may do the same, though the cheering crowds are definitely optional.

The annual PGA tournament is held at Pete Dye's beautiful Harbour Town Golf Links at Sea Pines in April, the week following the Master's Tournament in Augusta, Georgia. With spring flowers abounding, the setting is one of the most spectacular on the pro tour, and it is a favorite with fans, too.

You don't have to be a guest at Sea Pines to play the par 71, 6,652-yard course, though the greens fees are a little cheaper if you are. There are two other courses in Sea Pines: the Ocean Course, par 72, 6,614-yards, and Sea Marsh, par 72 and 6,372 yards. They are very nice, too. For information about playing Harbour Town or the other Sea Pines courses, call (800) 845-6131 or (843) 363-4485.

The Palmetto Dunes Resort in the middle of the island has three world-class courses. The Robert Trent Jones course is par 72 and plays at 6,707 yards; George Fazio's course is a par 70, 6,873-yard test; and the Arthur Hills-designed course is par 72 and measures 6,651 yards. All will challenge the ball control and accuracy of the best players. And as with the layouts in Sea Pines, these courses offer gorgeous vistas and handsomely sculpted greens. Call (800) 827-3006 for reservations or information.

Among the other popular and highly rated courses are the Arthur Hills–designed layout at Palmetto Hall, a 6,911, par 72 course; the Barony at Port Royal plantation, par 72, 6,530 yards; the Country Club of Hilton Head at Hilton Head plantation, par 72, 6,936 yards; the Golden Bear at Indigo

Run, designed by Nicklaus, which measures 7,014 and par 72; the Palmetto Hall–Robert Cupp course at Palmetto Hall Plantation, with par 72 and up to 7,079 yards; Planter's Row at Port Royal Plantation, par 72 and 6,520 yards; and Shipyard at Shipyard Plantation, which offers 27 holes on a George Cobb and Willard Byrd–designed layout.

All of the courses have fully stocked pro shops. All offer lessons and clinics for novices to the most experienced players.

There are other courses just a short drive or boat ride from the island. Ask the chamber of commerce for details, or check with your hotel or villa office. For information on the two courses at nearby Daufuskie Island, see the section following this one on Daufuskie.

Tennis

Hilton Head has been ranked annually by national magazines as one of America's top tennis resorts (in fact it was number one a couple of years ago). And with good reason. It claims more than three hundred courts of all surfaces, with the finest facilities to support them. The island is a familiar name in big-time tennis, too. For more than a quarter century the Family Circle Magazine Cup hosted the world's greatest women players here in March, including Chris Evert, Martina Navratilova, Steffi Graf, and Martina Hingis (the tournament moved to Charleston in 2001). And the men haven't been neglected, either. The likes of Stan Smith, Jimmy Connors, Bjorn Borg, and Pete Sampras have all played on these courts.

Tennis is taken very seriously. The courts are kept in great shape, play is offered day or night, and there are some of the finest pro shops anywhere, with lessons and clinics available year-round. Palmetto Dunes Tennis Center has twenty-five courts with clay and hard surfaces, eight of them lighted. The Sea Pines Racquet Club has twenty-eight courts, also clay and hard surfaces, with five of them lighted.

Other major tennis centers are found at the Van Der Meer Tennis Center, twenty-eight courts hard and clay, eight lighted; Van Der Meer Center at Shipyard, twenty clay and hard courts, eight with lights; and Port Royal Racquet Club at Port Royal Plantation, sixteen courts, clay, hard and grass, six lighted. Reservations are necessary; guests receive discounts. Check at your hotel or villa or when you are making your vacation reservations for details.

Recreation/Entertainment

Hilton Head is rightly famous for its magnificent white sand beaches. The beach is clean, the sand tightly packed, and it goes on and on (twelve miles of it). It's great for walking, biking, beachcombing, or just enjoying the sun and

In addition to the beaches at the island's resorts, Hilton Head has several public beaches with ample parking and access to the wide, white strand. (Courtesy Hilton Head Island Chamber of Commerce)

surf. There are few big waves here; don't plan on a very successful surfing expedition. South Beach in Sea Pines is probably best known and the island's widest beach. The area is a popular feeding ground for birds, gamefish, and dolphins. The beach in Port Royal Plantation is especially appealing as it curves around the island's heel, where the Atlantic meets Port Royal Sound. This was the site of Captain William Hilton's landing in 1663.

The island's four public beaches have parking and quick access to the water's edge. Starting at the northern end of the island and moving south, they may be found at Folly Field Beach on Folly Field Road; Driessen's Beach Park on Bradley Beach Road; Coligny Beach Park off Coligny Circle; and Forest

Beach off Forest Beach Road. There's no fee for using the public beaches, and you can walk up and down the beach as far as you wish, enjoying the ocean-side view of the expensive resort hotels and villas where guests are paying a lot more than you for the same view.

Anything you can do in the water can be done at Hilton Head. There are rentals for everything imaginable: rafts, canoes, kayaks, bikes, beach umbrellas, crabbing nets, scuba diving equipment, parasailing, and water skiing. If you want a boat, there are lots of choices: sailboat, motorboat, pontoon, or catamaran. Fishing boats may be chartered for full-day trips, or you can just pick up a small one for a little fishing in Calibogue Sound. Rental shops are all over the island. Just ask at your hotel or villa reservations office.

Bikes are a fun way to get around, and there are miles of bike paths. The public trails cover much of the middle of the island and are quite safe even with the high volume of traffic close by. The paths do not lead into private resort areas such as Sea Pines and Hilton Head Plantation (which have their own trails). Also available are rollerblades, tandem bikes, kiddie carts, and other wheeled variations.

Other options: an aerial tour of Hilton Head and the surrounding islands (offered at the airport, naturally); cruises around the island with opportunities for sightseeing and learning about the area's rich history; and horseback riding (two different stables offer rides for youngsters and adults).

Hilton Head has quite a lively and diverse arts community and a new state-of-the-art arts center that hosts most of the performing arts. The Self Family Arts Center opened in 1998 and welcomes a local symphony orchestra, ballet, art shows, and theatrical performances year-round. There are some excellent art galleries in the area. The world premiere of best-selling novelist John Jakes's musical adaptation of Charles Dickens' *Great Expectations* was staged here. Jakes, whose books include the well-known *North and South* trilogy, has made his home on the island for many years. For information about specific shows, call the center at (800) 842-ARTS or ask at your hotel or villa. Hilton Head residents are proud of this handsome facility at Shelter Cove on the middle of the island and are eager to talk about the cultural boost it has given the entire lowcountry.

There are plenty of nightclubs and lounges on the island, many with live evening entertainment every night during the summer and at least on weekends at other times. Check local calendars for who's appearing where.

Shopping

Shopping is very much a part of the Hilton Head experience for many visitors. The reasons why are simple: approximately five hundred retail locations on or close to the island and thirty different shopping areas. There are several discount outlets for some of the best-known names: Polo, Coach, Laura Ashley, Movado, J. Crew, Nike, and many others. The largest are two linked outlet malls on Highway 278 just before the Hilton Head bridge, called Hilton Head Factory Stores; prices are comparatively low for everything from perfumes to luggage to dresses, and crowds are large every day except on mid-winter weekdays.

The largest shopping area is Coligny Plaza, on the beach side near the middle of the island. More than sixty shops sell all manner of food, clothing, books, jewelry, liquor, shoes, hammocks, and toys. The Mall at Shelter Cove, in the middle of the island, has more than fifty upscale stores including Banana Republic, Belk, and Saks. There's an adjacent, attractive shopping and restaurant area at Shelter Cove Harbourside, and more dining and shopping options at the nearby Plaza at Shelter Cove.

Other major shopping areas are found at Orleans Plaza on New Orleans Road; Sea Pines Center in Sea Pines; Harbour Town (some nice boutiques); and Main Street Village, on the north part of the island near Hilton Head Plantation.

The resort hotels also have shopping areas featuring a variety of goods, from logo items to swimsuits, and high-end stock, from antiques to art.

There are many large, well-stocked grocery stores located throughout the island, always close to the Parkway.

The shopping areas stay busy year-round, but when it rains and no one can get out on the beaches, watch the cars heading for the malls. It's always shopping season here.

Daufuskie Island

After decades of virtual obscurity and isolation, known primarily for a book written about it in 1972 by novelist Pat Conroy, *The Water Is Wide* (made into a movie titled *Conrack*), Daufuskie at last has undergone a share of development. Even so, it retains some of its original character and quaintness because, unlike other sea islands, it does not have bridge access to the mainland.

The only way to get to Daufuskie is by private boat or passenger ferry, about a forty-minute journey from Hilton Head. Private boats depart from Harbour Town and the marinas, and there is a ferry from Salty Fare Village on the Skull Creek side of Hilton Head. To get to Salty Fare, cross over the 278 bridge to Hilton Head Island and continue about 1.5 miles on the William Hilton Parkway to Squire Pope Road. Take a left there to Salty Fare, which will be on your left just before the back gate to Hilton Head Plantation. Round-trip

Isolated Daufuskie Island is accessible by passenger ferry from Hilton Head or by private boat. (Courtesy South Carolina Department of Parks, Recreation & Tourism)

fare is $25 per person, and reservations are necessary; call (800) 648-6778. Ferry schedules vary with the season, with fewer trips in winter months. The journey to Daufuskie is one well worth making, even if you aren't planning to stay on the island.

Daufuskie is south of Hilton Head and just north of the Savannah River. You'll find there an exclusive residential community, Haig Point, and a relatively new development, the Daufuskie Island Club and Resort. That facility includes an oceanfront inn and cottages with lovely views of the beach and the marshes. There are plenty of activities for visitors, with two championship golf courses, a swimming pool, horseback riding, biking, and tennis. In addition, the resort boasts some fun watersports such as kayaking, parasailing, and dolphin watching. You can even catch up on your fly fishing in the island's lagoons and streams. The resort also has some special programs designed for youngsters during the day.

Those pursuits have little connection to the island's history. Daufuskie was not settled by the English until the mid-eighteenth century because of the threat to safety posed by the original inhabitants—the Indians—and troublesome Spanish raiders. Fierce clashes between the British and the Indians led to a series of bloody battles on the southern tip of Daufuskie which gave that part of the island the name Bloody Point. First indigo, then cotton, were the money crops after planters permanently settled here in the late eighteenth century. With the coming of Civil War and occupying Union soldiers, whites fled the island, leaving mostly slaves who were subsequently freed and many of whose descendants continued to live on the island through the twentieth century. Oystering, fishing, and farming provided modest livelihoods for the few remaining residents, black and white. While nearby islands underwent development, Daufuskie was ignored, largely for lack of access.

Conroy's book brought national attention to the island, detailing his teaching efforts to connect to the children of this remote Gullah culture and their parents, who lived in simple, rural conditions far removed from the comfortable conveniences of modern America. Declining economic opportunities forced increasing numbers of residents off the island, however, culminating in the purchase of portions of it for development in the final years of the twentieth century, bringing about the most dramatic changes in the island's long history.

As with other beach resorts along the South Carolina coast, summer is the high season here. But the high season also includes Thanksgiving and Christmas weeks and extends between March 15 and November 15. Comfortable inn rooms average $156 per night in high season, while two-bedroom cottages (four-bedroom units are available, too) are priced a little higher. Rates include breakfast and dinner and unlimited boat passage. Golf packages in high season range from $250 to $350 per night. At the Stoddard Room restaurant in the inn, the resort advises that "jackets are required for men and appropriate attire for ladies" during dinner hours.

The two golf courses on Daufuskie are first-rate. The Bloody Point course, a par 72, 6,900-yard layout set around marshlands and rolling terrain, was designed by Tom Fazio and Jay Morrish. The Jack Nicklaus–designed Melrose course is par 72, 7,081 yards with oceanside vistas on the magnificent and challenging finishing holes. Warning: if you're on the courses, or if you're outside at all, especially during the summer months, you'd better remember to bring bug repellent. Daufuskie's bugs can be fierce, and you will pay a price for your forgetfulness. The problem is worse inland.

A half-day trip around the non-resort areas of Daufuskie makes for a fascinating journey. A walk or travel on a golf cart will take you down a dirt road to the Mary Dunn Cemetery, where tombstones tell of the island's eighteenth-century residents. The First Union Baptist Church dates from 1880, and you can visit the 1912 small schoolhouse. It's a wondrous glimpse into the past, a little piece of sea island history still clinging to life amid the relentlessly golf-churned landscape of the coast.

Nine

Epilogue

From Little River, the coastline of South Carolina curves its graceful southwesterly way down to Daufuskie. You could drive (and boat) that entire coast easily in a day. Then again, you could visit the Grand Canyon for five minutes, too, but in neither case could you stretch your sketchy impressions into a serious perspective. Moving so quickly through this land that nature has caressed lovingly for centuries would miss the whole point: this is a place whose charm, whose energy, and whose soul is revealed only to those who choose to linger.

You can find seashells while walking on any beach in the state. But there's not a beach in South Carolina that is just like any other beach. The differences between the beach at Hunting Island and Myrtle Beach are as vast as the chasms of the Grand Canyon. They're each wonderfully unique environments of the lowcountry, but you're moving way too fast if you don't or can't see what separates them—and we're not talking about mileage.

In his 1986 best-selling novel *The Prince of Tides*, Pat Conroy, who has made his home for many years on Fripp Island, wrote of the power this land holds over him: "I am a patriot of a singular geography on the planet. I speak of my country religiously; I am proud of its landscape . . . my heart belongs in the marshlands." Even those who may lack the gift of such expression can grasp the feeling. All it takes is a visit. And a little time.

Reading List

Following are some suggestions for further reading of books written by authors who live along the South Carolina coast or by authors whose work is closely tied to the coast. It is not meant to be inclusive, but only to highlight some of my favorite and most helpful books.

Fiction

Baldwin, William. *The Hard to Catch Mercy.* Chapel Hill, N.C.: Algonquin Books, 1993.

———. *The Fennel Family Papers.* Chapel Hill, N.C.: Algonquin Books, 1996.

Battle, Lois. *Bed and Breakfast.* New York: Viking, 1996.

Bolick, Julian Stevenson. *The Return of the Gray Man, and Georgetown Ghosts.* Pawleys Island, S.C.: Jeptha, 1994.

Conroy, Pat. *The Water Is Wide.* Boston: Houghton Mifflin, 1972.

———. *The Great Santini.* Boston: Houghton Mifflin, 1976.

———. *The Prince of Tides.* Boston: Houghton Mifflin, 1986.

———. *Beach Music.* New York: Nan Talese/Doubleday, 1995.

Fox, William Price: *Lunatic Wind: Surviving the Storm of the Century.* Chapel Hill, N.C.: Algonquin Books, 1992.

Frank, Dorothea Benton. *Sullivan's Island: A Lowcountry Tale.* New York: Jove, 1999.

Godwin, Rebecca T. *Keeper of the House.* New York: St. Martin's Press, 1994.

Hamilton, Elizabeth Verner. *Storm Center.* Charleston, S.C.: Tradd Street Press, 1983.

Heyward, DuBose. *Porgy.* New York: George H. Doran, 1925.

———. *The Half Pint Flask.* New York: Farrar & Rinehart, 1929.

Humphreys, Josephine. *Dreams of Sleep.* New York: Viking, 1984.

———. *Rich in Love.* New York: Viking, 1987.

———. *The Fireman's Fair.* New York: Viking, 1991.

Huntsinger, Elizabeth. *Ghosts of Georgetown.* Winston-Salem, N.C.: John F. Blair, 1995.

———. *More Ghosts of Georgetown.* Winston-Salem, N.C.: John F. Blair, 1998.

Lott, Bret. *The Hunt Club.* New York: Villard, 1998.

Poe, Edgar Allan. "The Gold Bug" (1843). Available in *Collected Works of Edgar Allan Poe: Tales and Sketches, 1843–1849,* edited by Thomas Ollive Mabbott (Cambridge, Mass.: Belknap Press of Harvard University Press, 1978).

Powell, Padgett. *Edisto.* New York: Farrar, Straus & Giroux, 1984.

———. *Edisto Revisited.* New York: Henry Holt, 1996.

Sayers, Valerie. *Due East.* New York: Garden City, N.Y.: Doubleday, 1987.

———. *How I Got Him Back, or, Under the Cold Moon's Shine.* New York: Doubleday, 1989.

Siddons, Anne Rivers. *Low Country.* New York: HarperCollins, 1998.

Nonfiction

Ball, Edward. *Slaves in the Family.* New York: Farrar, Straus & Giroux, 1998.

Ballantine, Todd. *Tideland Treasure: The Naturalist's Guide to the Beaches and Salt Marshes of Hilton Head Island and the Southeastern Coast.* Columbia: University of South Carolina Press, 1991.

Burn, Billie. *An Island Named Daufuskie.* Spartanburg: The Reprint Company, 1991.

Cole, Nathan. *The Road to Hunting Island, South Carolina.* Charleston, S.C.: Arcadia, 1997.

Connor, Amy S., and Sheila L. Beardsley. *Edisto Island: A Family Affair.* Dover, N.H.: Arcadia Publishing, 1998.

Edgar, Walter. *South Carolina: A History.* Columbia: University of South Carolina Press, 1998.

Gragg, Rod. *Planters, Pirates and Patriots: Historical Tales from the South Carolina Grand Strand.* Nashville, Tenn.: Rutledge Hill Press, 1993.

———. *The Illustrated History of Horry County.* Myrtle Beach: Southern Communications, 1994.

Graydon, Nell S. *Tales of Beaufort.* Orangeburg, S.C.: Sandlapper, 1997.

———. *Tales of Edisto.* Orangeburg, S.C.: Sandlapper, 1986.

Green, Jonathan. *Gullah Images: The Art of Jonathan Green.* Columbia: University of South Carolina Press, 1996.

Harvey, Natalie (editor). *Hilton Head Island.* (Images of America series.) Charleston, S.C.: Arcadia, 1998.

Hess, Karen. *The Carolina Rice Kitchen: The African Connection.* Columbia: University of South Carolina Press, 1992.

Holmgren, Virginia. *Hilton Head: A Sea Island Chronicle.* Easley, S.C.: Southern Historical Press, 1986.

Jordan, Laylon Wayne, and Elizabeth H. Stringfellow. *A Place Called St. John's.* Spartanburg, S.C.: The Reprint Company, 1998.

Joyner, Charles. *Down by the Riverside*. Urbana: University of Illinois Press, 1984.

La Roche, Ramona. *Georgetown County, South Carolina*. (Black America Series.) Charleston, S.C.: Arcadia, 2000.

Lewis, Catherine H. *Horry County, South Carolina, 1730–1993*. Columbia: University of South Carolina Press, 1998.

Linder, Suzanne Cameron. *Historical Atlas of the Rice Plantations of the Ace River Basin, 1860*. Columbia: South Carolina Department of Archives and History, 1995.

Lindsay, Nick. *And I'm Glad: An Oral History of Edisto Island*. Charleston, S.C.: Tempus Publishing, 2000.

McClellanville Coast Cookbook. McClellanville, S.C.: privately printed, 1992.

Neuffer, Claude and Irene. *Correct Mispronunciations of Some South Carolina Names*. Columbia: University of South Carolina Press, 1983.

Pawleys Island Civic Association. *Pawleys Island, Historically Speaking*. Pawleys Island, S.C.: privately printed, 1994.

Peterkin, Genevieve, with William P. Baldwin. *Heaven Is a Beautiful Place: A Memoir of the South Carolina Coast*. Columbia: University of South Carolina Press, 2000.

Pringle, Elizabeth Allston. *A Woman Rice Planter*. Columbia: University of South Carolina Press, 1992.

Puckette, Clara Childs. *Edisto: A Sea Island Principality*. Johns Island, S.C.: Seaforth, 1978.

Rhyne, Nancy. *Chronicles of the South Carolina Sea Islands*. Winston-Salem, N.C.: John F. Blair, 1998.

Rogers, George C., Jr. *The History of Georgetown County*. Columbia: University of South Carolina Press, 1970.

Rose, Willie Lee. *Rehearsal for Reconstruction: The Port Royal Experiment*. Indianapolis, Ind.: Bobbs-Merrill, 1964.

Rowland, Lawrence C., et al. *The History of Beaufort County, Volume 1, 1514–1861*. Columbia: University of South Carolina Press, 1996.

Rutledge, Archibald. *Hunting and Home in the Southern Heartland: The Best of Archibald Rutledge*. Edited by Jim Casada. Columbia: University of South Carolina Press, 1992.

―――. *Home by the River*. Orangeburg, S.C.: Sandlapper, 1983.

Vaughan, Celina McGregor. *Pawleys . . . As It Was*. Columbia, S.C.: R. L. Bryan, 1998.

Williams, Susan, ed. *McClellanville Coast Seafood Cookbook*. McClellanville, S.C.: McClellanville Arts Council, 1996.

Index

Boldface entries denote extended discussion of a particular beach.